WHY DON'T THEY BELIEVE US?

Philip Fogarty SJ

Why don't they believe us?

HANDING ON THE FAITH
IN A CHANGING SOCIETY

THE COLUMBA PRESS
DUBLIN 1993

First edition, 1993, published by
THE COLUMBA PRESS
93 The Rise, Mount Merrion, Blackrock, Co Dublin

ISBN 1 85607 084 0

Cover by Bill Bolger
Origination by The Columba Press
Printed in Ireland by
Colour Books Ltd., Dublin

Contents

For Peter-Paul

Introduction

Many young people, and especially those living in the poorer areas of Irish cities, are voting with their feet. They are often alienated from the Church and have given up on the sacraments. Many parents are dismayed because their children have stopped going to church, fail to have their children baptised, or live together without bothering about a church wedding.

I have heard parents blame themselves and wonder where they have gone wrong. I have heard Churchmen blame the lack of 'proper religious instruction', as if all the fault lay with teachers. Teachers sense the malaise but are uncertain as to the real nature of the problem. They feel that if they can improve their catechetical programmes and liturgies, or find some other magic formula, all will be well. But after all their efforts in recent years, they must begin to wonder.

'Religion, well I can't see the point of it all. Going to church is so boring and I certainly can't buy all that the Church teaches about contraception and sex before marriage. Of course I am not interested. I can't be bothered, it's true. What's the point?' is a typical reaction. This could easily be dismissed as normal teenage rebellion, and yet it does raise some fundamental questions about young people and their faith, and the relevance of the education they are receiving in schools today.

The problems faced by parents and by schools today have as much to do with the present state of society, the nature of our educational system, and the 'privatisation' of religion, as they do with any-

7

thing parents or teachers do or fail to do. Having participated in the changes that have come about in Church and State over the last thirty years or so and, as a school Principal for some fifteen years, agonised about the way these changes have affected our young people's faith, I would like to share something of my own faith journey over these years, reflect on the changes that have come about in society, and suggest ways that we might go about dealing with the challenges we now face.

Many people know that there is more to life than 'getting and spending', and are searching for meaning and a sense of purpose which I believe the Church and Christian schools can offer, if they honestly try to follow in Christ's footsteps. But that is the heart of the matter. Are we genuinely following in the Master's footsteps?

Philip Fogarty SJ

PART I

Rediscovering Christianity

CHAPTER 1

A Time for Questioning

When I was young, our family lived next door to the local Bishop, a very formidable figure. I remember my brother tangling with him in an episode that reveals the spirit of the times well. As a student, my brother developed tuberculosis and spent some time in a local sanitorium. To while away the hours he decided to write a letter to the *Irish Times*, exhorting the Church to allow Catholics to enter Trinity College which they were then forbidden to do under pain of mortal sin. Some days after the letter appeared, the Bishop's secretary arrived at his bedside with a message from the Bishop condemning the content of the letter and urging a return to right thinking. Some months later, after my brother returned home, he chased his golden labrador over the wall of our house into the bishop's property and encountered the man himself out for a walk. 'Young man,' said the Bishop, 'are you the fellow that wrote that letter to the newspaper about Trinity College?' 'Yes,' my brother replied. 'Tell me, young man, what side was Trinity College on in our fight for independence?'. My brother looked him straight in the eye and replied, 'The same side as the Bishops, my Lord!' The Bishop turned and walked away and my brother came home to tell my mother what he had said. She wondered whether excommunication was on the cards!

In the Ireland of the forties and fifties, Bishops tended to pronounce weightily on such matters as dancing during Lent or the evils of mixed bathing. It is hard today to conceive of the awe and fear in which Bishops or parish priests were held in those adolescent days of Irish nationhood. To challenge a Bishop was to play with fire.

In the fifties, Irish society was still relatively insular and stable and the Church's influence was all-pervasive. At school, I was nourished on the twin faiths of Catholicism and Nationalism. Nationalism meant some degree of faith in the Irish language and a narrow sense of cultural identity that was fostered through the educational system. My Catholicism grew out of a family tradition that accepted Church-going and family prayer as a normal part of life. My belief in God and in the Church reflected the relatively simple, though profound, faith of my parents. A short poem by my father gives something of its flavour.

Lord, give me a quiet mind, a happy heart
Content to dwell apart in humble places
With humble men of simple Faith,
Close to nature and the fruitful earth;
To see, with vision sharpened by simplicity,
The Wisdom and the all-sustaining Love of the Creator:
In quietude and peace to hear the voice of God.

I entered religious life in nineteen fifty seven with the idea of trying to 'win souls for Christ and bringing people back to the Sacraments'. At the same time I tried to build a relationship with Christ in the depths of my own heart. My faith had little to do with the larger social, political or economic issues of the day. Very soon, however, things were to change, especially with the election of Pope John XXIII and the second Vatican Council when the wider world began to impinge and, for the first time I began to question my faith. Even the language of Christianity began to puzzle me with its talk of Salvation and Grace, Redemption and Salvation. What had such things to say to my life as a university student or later as a student of philosophy and theology?

After two years in the monastic seclusion of a novitiate, as I began to mix once more with my contemporaries in University College Dublin, I found that many of them were alienated from the religion of their school days and were experiencing a growing alienation from the Church. They were uncertain and doubtful about the relevance of their religious education to the cut and

11

thrust of daily living. Many had a sneaking feeling that there was more to life than 'getting and spending'. They tried to cope in different ways. Some packaged life into neat compartments, seeing the weekly round of work and leisure as having little or no connection with Sunday worship. 'I struggle to go to Mass and perhaps, if my arm is twisted, I add some other 'good works' during the week but by and large my daily life and my 'Church' life remain mostly separate'. Others felt that if the demands of everyday life were so at odds with the demands of the Church, it was more honest to let 'Church practice' go and they drifted away from all contact with religion. Some felt that there was a need to find some ways of relating religion and life but they did not know how or where.

My own religious faith at this time was still a very private affair between myself and God. It had to do with obedience to the Church in order to ensure my eternal salvation and of bringing others to the faith so that they too might be saved. It engendered many fears: of bad thoughts, of sexual sin, of bad confessions. It meant saying the Rosary and going to Mass and Confession. Christian faith, as I understood it, was all about keeping rules and getting into heaven.

My early years as a Jesuit allowed me to question the faith in fairly safe surroundings. There was always people or books to whom I could turn. In this I was in a more fortunate position than many of my contemporaries. But as some questions were answered more began to surface.

A number of experiences over the next few years had a profound effect on me. Many of my contemporaries started leaving religious life and some of my relations were beginning to drift away from the Church causing me a sense of deep unease. The Church had become too authoritarian for their liking or they found its ceremonies more and more meaningless. I began to wonder how the Church could cope with so many young people who were voting with their feet. Then in the 1970's I spent some time living in a flat in Liverpool and working with unemployed youngsters in Toxteth in the aftermath of race riots in the city. Many of the young people I met had been involved in those riots, hurling stones at the police. They were mostly black and unemployed and saw no future for themselves in British society. In no sense were they Church-goers, though the centre where they met was run by a priest who did what he could for them by providing a meeting place and by trying to get them some employment. The Church was present to them but present in a very different way from anything I had experienced before. I found myself apprehensive in their presence. I would spend long hours drinking tea and listening to their experiences of life on the streets of Liverpool. After a while I began to wonder what I was doing there and asked my priest friend. His reply: 'Just listen to them. That is all you have to do!' I had the urge to be up and doing but what was there to do. So for hours on end I sat and listened and as I did so I began to learn something about a side of life that was totally new to me. I learned about the frustrations of being young and black in Liverpool, of being unemployed and of possibly never having a job. When the time came for me to leave, I was told that I had done well! I had listened and been accepted. I had come to the group feeling that I could do something for them but in the end it was they who did something for me. I had learned from the poor something of what it means to be poor. No one else could have taught me that. The experience also had another effect: it forced me back to the gospels so that I began to question them in a new way.

Some years later the same questions were forced to the forefront of my consciousness. Over several Sundays, I accompanied a Jesuit colleague of mine on visits to a bario or shanty town in Manila, capital of the Philippines. We entered the bario through a small unobtrusive gate at the side of a main road. To our left was a high wall of a well-to-do home. Against this wall were rough shacks made of light timber or corrugated sheets as far as the eye could see. There was a narrow mud footpath and more shacks to the right built over a stream that served as toilet, sewer and waste disposal unit. The shacks were closely packed in a maze of twisting and turning mud alleyways: homes to some five hundred families or over three thousand people. It was one of hundreds of such barios around Manila. As we walked along the mud footpath, groups of young men were playing pool on a makeshift table while others stood around chatting and drinking San Miguel beer. There were a few tiny shack stores selling crisps, coke, vegetables and beer. In the mud alleyway a young man was having his hair cut; a mother was bathing her baby, while another woman was trying to wash clothes. There was no privacy in that crowded ghetto. Most people were jobless. A few drove jeepneys (a sort of mini bus) for the relatively well off in the city. Others tried to sell flowers or cigarettes on the heavily polluted streets of Manila. We came to a small chapel with a tin roof and three bare concrete walls. It was full of small children. A choir of youngsters was getting ready for Mass. A small number of adults arrived. Numbers at Mass varied each week depending on whether or not there had been a drinking party in the bario the night before. The Mass was in Tagalog, the local language. A young ex-seminarian preached. There was much singing and the whole affair was strangely joyful and moving.

Families in the shanty included relatives who came in from the countryside and moved in with their city cousins. One woman I spoke to had lived there for thirteen years with no hope of ever having a real home of her own. The people were very friendly and welcoming and 'honoured' by having a visiting priest from Ireland. They seemed to survive by sharing what little they have with each other. They had discovered wells in the area from which their 'clean' water was drawn and some had even found ways of tapping illegally into the local electricity supply. They have no hospitals, medical care, welfare institutions or dole. They are the poorest of the poor beyond anything I had imagined.

Visiting the bario brought home, in very vivid fashion, the great disparities of wealth and poverty that exists on the globe. The words of Jesus came back to me 'Happy are you poor, the Kingdom of God is yours'. I felt that in the bario I was in touch with

14

something essential to Christianity, something I did not find else-where. Yet I could not help wondering whether what Jesus had promised was not just 'pie in the sky when you die'. His promises seemed unreal and even shocking in that shanty town. I wondered what today's poor would make of his words; the unemployed, the homeless, the starving millions in a world of plenty, those caught up in rich men's wars, maimed and killed by napalm bombs and guns produced from the rich man's table. These were and are disturbing questions and they forced me to look again at my rather cosy understanding of Christianity, at the faith of my fathers.

My life was and in many ways still is very middle class. While never knowing wealth, I have certainly never experienced real poverty. Today I still have meals on the table, I am surrounded by books. I profess to be a follower of Jesus of Nazareth, a poor man from Galilee, yet how little I know him. It is hard enough to know and understand one's friends not to mention oneself. How much harder still it is to know someone who lived in a society and at a time so very different from our own with its different customs, language and outlook on life. I was forced to rethink my Christianity, to go back across the centuries to try to understand the carpenter's son from Nazareth and see what relevance, if any, he has not only for me and the people I mix with but for those who welcomed me so warmly in Liverpool or Manila.

15

CHAPTER 2

A Time for Searching

Having studied theology, I might be expected to know at least some of the answers to the perplexing questions raised by my experience, but the rather esoteric discussions on the nature of Grace or Eschatology, Salvation or Ecclesiology, somehow did not seem real when compared to the lived experiences of Manila's poor. Theology can be pursued in a rather rarified atmosphere unrelated to the lived experiences of the poor or the ordinary lay person. I am reminded again of my father who wrote a poem in the thirties at a time when there was some discussion about revising the *Prayer Book* of the Established Church.

> *The Canon says: 'Yes'*
> *And the Dean says: 'No'*
> *And the Curate says: 'Both are wrong.'*
> *And away they all go*
> *(With a Hey nonny no!)*
> *To the service of Evensong.*
>
> *The Bishop says: 'Aye'*
> *And the Canon says: 'Nay'*
> *And the Curate says: 'Couple of frauds.'*
> *And away they all go*
> *(With a Hey nonny no!)*
> *To the service of Matins and Lauds.*
>
> *The Canon, the Bishop, the Curate, the Dean,*
> *Arm in arm to church they go.*
> *But the world and his wife*
> *Keep out of the strife*
> *And go to a Picture Show!*

Manila and Liverpool forced me out of the cul de sac of seminary and purely abstract thought and back to Jesus and beyond in order to find what I was looking for in the present. To understand my religion I had to rethink everything I had been taught so as to understand the values that Jesus lived by and see how they could apply in my own life and in modern Irish society.

My limited experience of poverty in Ireland and England, not to mention the poverty and starvation in the Third World, forced me to face my complacency and question many of my middle class values. At the same time I began to read the Bible in a way that helped to clarify much that up to then had seemed strange to me. When I began to look at Jesus of Nazareth and notice his identification with the poor, what had seemed merely a promise of 'pie in the sky when you die' took on a new and more immediate meaning.

To understand any man one needs to know something of his background and culture. Jesus was a Jew and Jewish history was built on the twin pillars of the Law and the Prophets. Jesus spoke and acted like the Jewish prophets of old. A prophet was not someone who foretold the future but a person who could read the signs of history, could interpret what was happening in his time and compare it to what God wanted of his people. The prophets were people of great insight who warned their compatriots what would happen them if they did not change their ways. Of course, since few of us like to hear bad news about ourselves, the prophetic message was often scorned and the prophets put to death.

The Jewish people saw God as one who delivered them, time after time, from whatever oppression was imposed on them. He was their Saviour. They understood that he made agreements or covenants with them and stuck to those agreements. In return he wanted his people to worship him and him alone. But the worship they were to give him was not just the traditional worship of offering sacrifices. What caught my attention was something that linked into my experience in Liverpool and Manila. God revealed that he wanted to be worshipped by the promotion of justice.

17

While God was the Saviour, the people were to be his instruments of that salvation. The words of the prophet Amos jumped off the pages for they struck a very modern note. 'Listen to this, you who trample on the needy and try to suppress the poor people of the country, you who say 'when will New Moon be over so that we can sell our corn, and Sabbath so that we can harvest our wheat? Then by lowering the bushel, raising the shekel, by swindling and tampering with the scales, we can buy up the poor for money, and the needy for a pair of shoes and get a price even for the sweepings of the wheat'. Or Isaiah: 'Take your wrongdoing out of my sight. Cease to do evil. Learn to do good. Search for justice, help the oppressed, be just to the orphan, plead for the widow'. The theme of justice as the way to worship God is a constant one in the Prophets and Psalms of the Jewish Testament. 'He (the King) will free the poor man who calls on him, and those who need help: he will have pity on the poor and feeble, and save the lives of those in need; he will redeem their lives from exploitation and outrage, their lives will be precious in his sight', Psalm 72 says. What struck me in the Prophetic writings was the regard that God had for all men and women. Each person is due the respect that is his or hers as a child of God, but, above all, respect is to be given to the poorest of the poor who are especially dear to the heart of God. When I think back to those people I met in the Bario in Manila and the greed and self-interest of the landlords and politicians that keeps them in their destitution, I hear the call of God ringing out anew in our own time: a call to all of us, as the instruments of his salvation, to do what we can to make the world a place fit for human habitation.

When I turned to the Christian Scriptures, I found Jesus following in the same prophetic tradition. It was then that I began to discover that much of what I thought I understood about Jesus began to unravel. As I reflected on my Christian beliefs and on the fact that so many of my own contemporaries, as well as the young people I dealt with on a year by year basis, were leaving the Church or were apathetic towards Christianity, I was forced to go back to the Scriptures to see whether I had got things wrong.

The Letter to the Hebrews describes Jesus as 'the radiant light of God's glory and the perfect copy of his nature.' Jesus the man revealed God; let us know what he is really like, and it was this man that the first disciples came to know and, after the resurrection, gradually thought of as being divine. So if I was to understand God's ways, I had to come to know Jesus in his humanity.

My education had taught me to think of Jesus as God, as a miracle worker who was more than human. Without denying his divinity, it was important for me not to forget what the Church has always said about him, that he was fully human; that he had to grow in wisdom like everyone else; that he could get sick, feel tired, get angry, experience the joys and sorrows of family and village life as much as anyone else; experience dejection and defeat; that he was not all seeing and knowing but saw the world from a particular, if especially insightful, point of view. He was limited by his time and place and culture and it was from within that culture that he revealed what God is like.

I also discovered another remarkable fact. Jesus was a carpenter's son and carpenters were by no means at the bottom of the social scale. Jesus, in modern terms, was a middle class man. His birth and upbringing meant that he was not one of the poor or the oppressed. After he left home he choose to mix socially with the poorest and most deprived of his time and identify with them. People like Mother Teresa or Jean Vanier in our own time have done the same.

The driving force in Jesus' life was compassion. He saw around him people who were very poor or who were treated as outsiders in society: beggars, the blind, the deaf, cripples, lepers, unskilled labourers, slaves as well as widows and orphans who had no one to care for them and so had to beg to survive. They all lacked status, honour and prestige, things highly valued in Jewish society. As a result, they felt humiliated and even abandoned by God. They regarded themselves as 'sinners' and were so described by the Scribes and Pharisees because they could not keep the many minutiae of the Jewish Law. Jesus' heart went out to those suffering people, arousing in him a deep compassion and he determined to do something about their plight. I'm sure he would feel the same today about those who suffer in the barios of Manila, who starve in Somalia or are forced to live on the borders of Irish society through poverty and unemployment since such people too feel themselves outcasts. 'Being unemployed', an unemployed person has said, 'is like being a leper. People draw back from you.'

Jesus spoke about bringing Good News to the people of his own time. Good News is always news about eliminating something feared, something dangerous, freedom from some oppression, suffering or evil or about something good that gives people courage and hope for the future. Jesus' Good News was good news for everybody, but in the first place it was good news for the poor!

The Good News that Jesus brought was startling. He claimed that God was not some remote, angry or uninterested deity but a loving Father whom we could address as 'Abba', 'Dad'. Jesus went further and said that the Father was immediately and intimately present now among us, was one with us provided that we 'repented'. By 'repentance' he did not mean some sort of self-flaggelation for our sins but a new way of thinking and acting. He wanted people to change their lives into lives of justice and mercy towards others, especially the poor, because for him, as for the prophets before him, this was the proper way to worship God and bring salvation to the world. When people respond to God by living lives of love, justice and mercy towards others then they are helping to bring into existence what Jesus called the Kingdom of God. God reigns in the world, Jesus said, when truth and justice, mercy and love exist, especially for the poor and the oppressed.

Hans Kung puts it this way: 'Jesus did not demand and still less set in motion a politico-social revolution. What he did set going was a decidedly non-violent revolution: a revolution emerging from man's innermost and secret nature, from the personal centre, from the heart of man, into society. There was to be no continuing in the old ways, but a radical change in man's thinking and a conversion (Gk. *metanoia*), away from all forms of selfishness, toward God and his fellow man. The real alien powers, from which man had to be liberated, were not the hostile world powers but the forces of evil: hatred, injustice, dissension, violence, all human selfishness and also suffering, sickness and death. There had to be therefore a changed awareness, a new way of thinking, a new scale of values. The evil that had to be overcome lay not only in the system, in the structures, but in man. Inner freedom had to be established and this would lead to freedom from external powers. Society had to be transformed through the transformation of the individual. (*On Being a Christian*, Collins, London, 1977. p 191).

Jesus asked his followers, as did the Prophet Micah, to act justly, love tenderly and walk humbly with God. This is what Jesus himself did. He freed the sick from their illnesses and dispelled the fear of demons but, above all, he gave back to the poor and the oppressed a sense of their dignity as human beings and a knowledge that they were beloved of God. He went further by arguing with Israel's rulers about their religious regulations which bore down so hard on the poor. He even took on business interests by staging a demonstration in the temple, driving out the traders and money lenders who were making God's house into a 'den of thieves'. In effect Jesus challenged all oppressors by appealing to them to have a change of heart. The Father, he said, was a God of love and all men and women as children of the Father were entitled to justice and love. Jesus' abiding passion was to bring about the Kingdom of God where all men and women could live in solidarity as brothers and sisters, as children of a loving God. This was the Good News, the gospel he preached.

21

CHAPTER 3

A Time for Conversion

As I ponder what Jesus said and did, I am still startled by his message that God dwells among men and women here in our world. Jesus did not envisage two contrasting worlds, the sacred and the profane, the spiritual and the human. The sacred or spiritual seems to be 'above' and 'beyond' ordinary day-to-day living. Yet Jesus said quite clearly that God is to be found, not in some world above, but in the concrete realities of daily living. I am to find God in all things here on earth. My tendency all the time is to move from the human to a different, sacred level; to try to find God 'above' human interaction and seek to placate or manipulate him with prayer or sacred rites. But God has paid humanity the compliment of allowing himself to be found in the midst of human preoccupations. To feed the hungry, to receive the stranger, to clothe the naked, to visit prisoners, is to find God in the world. *(Mt 25)*

To find God, however, requires conversion and this means more than accepting doctrines or dogmas. If I am to find God, Jesus says, I have to repent, that is have a change of priorities and a change of outlook in my life. This is where I find the stumbling blocks because, for many reasons, I may not wish to change the way I think or the way I live. My old ways of looking at life give me a certain security that is hard to let go. Over the years I have developed certain prejudices and loyalties that have to do with race, nationality, language, family, religious denomination, class or political party. Like my contemporaries, I have given special value to people with position, power and wealth. But the way Jesus looked on all these is very different from the way that I tend to see them and 'conversion' means coming to see them as Jesus did and acting in regard to them as he did: no easy matter!

Some years ago two Italian journalists came to see me. They were doing a story about James Joyce and were visiting one of the schools where he had been educated. After discussing Joyce's school days, one of them suddenly asked me: 'What did you have to do to become Headmaster of such a prestigious school?' The question made me think. Yes, I was the principal of a famous school. My opinions were looked for. If I wrote to the papers my letters were published. I had been mentioned on the Gay Byrne show, interviewed on radio and even been quoted in the editorial column of the Irish Times! I certainly had status and position and was regarded as a valued member of society accordingly. What, I wondered, would Jesus have made of such status and position? His fame was very limited in his own time. He was known to the authorities late in his career as a troublemaker and a rabble-rouser. The ordinary people flocked to him but he was despised by those with any real power or influence. He was a man who identified himself with the poor and the oppressed. He did not own a home or have an office or headquarters. He was at the mercy of others and had to meet people on the roads, in the market place, in boats or in the temple. He lacked social standing. Having identified with the poor, he did not enjoy the power that came from wealth. In terms of the power structures of his day, he was powerless, overlooked, set aside, forgotten, looked down on, despised, ridiculed. He shared the loneliness and isolation, the vulnerability and insecurity of the poor.

In Jesus' time the Jewish class system was rigid. Position and status in society were indicated by the way one dressed and was spoken to and by whom one entertained and by where one sat in the synagogue. Status and position are still important in our society. They are determined by a person's education, income and the respect that one is paid by society. I was once invited to a party by a friend of mine, an auctioneer in Dublin. The country was going through a bout of economic decline and he had decided to hold an 'anti-gloom' party! I was introduced by name only to a group of people whom I had never met before. They were in the middle of a discussion about the economic state of the country. They discussed the rise and fall of the pound and the current state of share prices. Occasionally my opinions were elicited and I made some non-committal comments that sought to hide my ignorance. The discussion turned to boats. One of the group had recently purchased a large boat which he was planning to use as a cruiser on the Shannon. During a lull in the conversation, I was asked my profession and I confined myself to stating that I was a teacher. This was greeted with some surprise and sympathy! The conversation quickly turned to other matters as though I had lowered the tone of the conversation. Soon afterwards I had to leave but some weeks later was talking to my friend again and he regaled me with the subsequent drift of conversation at the party. As soon as I had left the room he was asked about 'the teacher'. When he said that I was a Jesuit and the headmaster of a famous school the tone changed. I was now someone with standing: someone who mattered! Even among these financiers and bankers I could find a place. Jesus' words came back to me. Describing the Scribes and Pharisees, he said: 'Everything they do is done to attract attention, like wearing broader phylacteries and longer tassels, like wanting to take the place of honour at banquets and the front seats in the synagogues, being greeted obsequiously in the market squares and having people call them Rabbi'. Jesus saw that judging people according to their social position falsifies human relationships because some are seen as more important than others, more deserving of respect and even of subservience: it devalues the human person by making the wealthy or those with social standing of more importance than the poor, the handicapped, the outcasts of society thus marginalising them. Jesus said: 'I tell you solemnly, unless you become like little children you will never enter the Kingdom of heaven'. Jesus had no illusions about the so-called innocence of youth but he took 'the little ones' as living symbols of those who were not among the great and prestigious and yet were to be valued for what they were: sons and daughters of 'Abba' from whom they derive their dignity.

In many ways Jesus turns my way of looking at the world upside down compelling me to rethink my values as regards my fellow human beings, my family, politics, even my nationality and race. I am to love my enemies, do good to those who hate me, bless those who curse me, pray for those who treat me badly. I am to 'hate' father, mother, wife, children, brothers, sisters and even my own life if I am to be his disciple! (Commentators point out that due to the poverty of Hebrew and Aramaic languages, the word 'hate' can cover many meanings including indifference, not preferring etc. The latter is Jesus' meaning). Jesus wanted people not to be selective in their love; not just to love family and friends or a particular group or nation but all those who come one's way because they too are sons and daughters of 'Abba'. Family and friends are to be loved because they too are children of God but not to the exclusion of anyone else, particularly the poor. Jesus was looking for a new, universal solidarity that would replace old exclusive groupings that excluded some or sought to make them feel inferior in any way. This way of looking at things may help to explain how Jesus related to his own family. One reads in the gospel how his relations thought that Jesus was out of his mind. 'His mother and his brothers now arrived and, standing outside, sent in a message asking for him. A crowd was sitting round him at the time the message was passed to him. 'Your mother and brothers and sisters are outside looking for you'. He replied, 'Who are my mother and my brothers?' And looking at those sitting in the circle about him, he said 'here are my mother and brothers. Anyone who does the will of God, that person is my brother and sister and mother.' Jesus' love for his mother was not based simply on biological or family connections but because she too followed the will of God by loving with a non-exclusive love.

Jesus looked for a new, universal solidarity to replace old exclusive groupings. I prefer to mix with my own kind and remain suspicious of those who differ from me in race, language, social class, religion, colour or politics. From early on in life, I have built up my own map of the world: a way of seeing it and understanding it and giving it meaning. This has been conditioned by family, friends, schooling, Church and my social environment generally as well as by the choices I have made in life. Possessing such a map also provides me with security and so I am slow to change it, to realise that there are other islands of knowledge, other ways of thinking about things, of evaluating them, of doing things that are different from mine. There are other, equally valid, cultures. Jesus said that to be a follower of his one had to change one's map of life and above all to see it from the perspective of the poor and the oppressed. When I realise that all men and women are brothers and sisters, children of the same Father and yet that many are hungry, deprived, persecuted, tortured or suffering, then my heart is changed, my perspective on life altered, my desire to do something about injustice is set alight. To see life from the perspective of the poor is challenging and frightening and is why conversion is such a slow process. While Jesus loved all those who came into his life, he particularly extended his compassion to the poor and despised in order to restore in them a sense of worth and dignity that society had removed. Since he was regarded as a man of God, moving in their company made them feel accepted by God and restored their faith in themselves. It was to the outcasts that Jesus brought his good news first. I can only understand that good news if I become 'poor in spirit'!

On a personal level, then, I discovered that what Jesus had to say about God and about the world was quite different from what I had been taught. My map of reality was being extended once more in a slow, painful process. This happened in two ways: on one hand I came to realise that I had not fully understood the extent of the conversion of mind and heart that Jesus spoke of and on the other I realised that Jesus' teaching was addressed to me not just as an individual but as a member of society. Christ's message was not a private revelation to me for my own personal, selfish salvation, i.e. escape from hell or purgatory. His teaching had social as well as personal implications which I needed to tease out. How could what happened two thousand years ago have any relevance for me today and what did it have to say to a modern Ireland? This question brought me back to the relevance of Christianity for young people who start from themselves, their own experience of the world, their own searching. For many today and especially for young people, faith is not just a question of arguing from abstract ideas and principles but of speaking from one's own experience and speaking to their experience, otherwise it is not credible. It must speak to today's joys and sorrows, today's pain and challenge. If faith simply refers to something that happened in the distant past once-for-all it can hardly be relevant to life today: it can hardly be called Good News for modern men or women.

So often faith is just seen as a set of beliefs, a collection of prayers, a series of rituals, of moral do's and dont's, that do not seem to relate directly to one's day-to-day experience. Young people start from their experience and today people are rediscovering the value of experience and how God speaks to us through it. God has spoken to humanity in the past through the historical experience of people. This is called Revelation. The written gospels, doctrines and traditions of the past (the deposit of faith) are normative and authoritative in the sense that what I have experienced as God's activity in my life, or in the life of my community, must 'square' with the ways God acted in the past. But God still makes himself known today through human experience. When God's Spirit, welling up from the unconscious as it were, opens our eyes, when we begin to see life from God's perspective, then we begin to see things very differently. A friend of mine has fostered three severely handicapped children who are now in their teen years. At times life gets too much for her. 'Life is not fair' she cries when the burden of caring becomes too much for her. It is a hard day-in-day-out burden to have to minister to all the physical as well as psychological needs of such handicapped youngsters with virtually no help from the state. 'Why does God let this happen to me?' is a common cry. Yet, at other moments, she sees the joy and bubbling enthusiasm for life in those children and at such moments she sees life differently. It becomes, even if only for a while, a source of pleasure and a rewarding struggle. The facts have not changed, but the way she sees them has. If she were to see the

27

strength, courage and commitment she brings to caring for those children as God-given then she would be having what is called a religious experience. She would bring God into the picture.

A religious experience is not just some enormous moment of revelation from on high but any experience in which I bring God into the picture. When I am overawed by the beauty of sea or mountain; when I choose courage in the face of adversity, commitment in the face of uneven odds, strength when faced with a calamity, love when selfishness would rather prevail, I am having a religious experience for I see these as God-given powers, going beyond anything that I could achieve by myself. Some people will be content to classify these experiences as human experiences but since I find God in all that is most human they are more for me than that. It is a matter of how one sees the world: with or without the eyes of faith.

Many young people see religion as being concerned primarily with morality or ethics. But it means more than that: it even has to do with more than just loving one's neighbour. It has to do with the way we see the world, about the meaning of our times, about the significance of what is happening now, about what God is doing in and through human beings in the present. 'I can't prove to you that a human life is special and of unique value, anymore than someone else can prove that it isn't. I can only suggest to you that some wonderful and liberating things (and also some difficult and demanding things) happen to you when you come to see life through the eyes of religious faith. I can only suggest that there is something innate in each of us that responds to the idea that human life is sacred. When we have learned to see life religiously, we will understand why we have certain commitments that have no basis in logic or science: that the birth of a child is something wonderous, worthy of celebration, and that the death of a child is a searing tragedy; that it makes sense to spend thousands of dollars and hundreds of man-hours to rescue one person from a collapsed building; that an elderly widow has a right to enjoy life and not be left alone to await her own death ... I can't prove to you that any of these statements are true. I can only tell you that when you have learned to see the world in a certain way, you will accept them without requiring proof, and one of the lives whose specialness you will come to believe in is your own.' (*Who Needs God*, Harold Kushner, Simon and Shuster, 1990. p 30)

People are gradually beginning to revalue and trust human experience where before abstract ideas and principles dominated our lives and human experience was regarded as very unreliable. Of course I have to reflect on my experience and see its limitations. In doing this with others I have a better chance of broadening my insights and if I do it in the light of the gospels and the deposit of faith I can begin to see whether it is consonant with the way God acts in the world; whether it can be classified as a religious experience or not.

If the gospel is to mean anything to young people it has to take into account their experience of life in present-day Ireland. To do otherwise, to pretend that it refers only to something that happened in the dim and distant past, in ancient history, or that it is merely a series of rituals or of moral do's and dont's, is to make it irrelevant. The Good News must be good news now, otherwise it is nothing.

The problems that Jesus confronted were not just those of a particular individual, a particular person's illness or guilt or selfishness. Jesus also faced up to the wider problems of his society: the occupation of his country by a foreign power; the greed, abuse of money and power by sections of society as well as the abuse of the Law to dominate people's lives. He not only healed the sick and cured the leper, he also challenged the social mores of his time and was put to death for his pains. He challenged society by challenging individuals to change so that they could, with others, transform society.

Like the Prophets before him, Jesus read the Signs of the Times and urged repentance, a change of heart and mind. 'When you see a cloud looming up in the west you say at once that rain is coming, and so it does. And when the wind is from the south you say it will be hot, and it is. Hypocrites! You know how to interpret the face of the earth and sky. How is it that you do not know how to interpret these times?' *(Lk 12:54-56).* For Jesus the ordinary events of life: the effects of Roman imperialism, the hypocrisy of the religious establishment and the consequent misery and oppression of the poor cried out for justice, the way to worship God. Jesus saw poverty and suffering in relation to God. They were not just human experiences but religious ones. God was on the side of the poor and the oppressed, as he always had been in the history of Israel, striving through Jesus, as he had through the Prophets before him, to free the poor from their misery and oppression. God, in Jesus, was demonstrating to his people how they could find true freedom from their oppression, misery and all that kept them enslaved if they underwent a radical conversion of heart and mind.

Today people are called to read the signs of our times for Christ continues to challenge the Irish way of life. His call for radical conversion that I as an individual must undergo if I am to make any significant contribution towards perfecting the world, (towards building the Kingdom) still stands. But the gospel also challenges our corporate responsibility for the situation in Northern Ireland, the treatment meted out to the poor, the homeless, the sick, the disabled, the more than 270,000 unemployed, to emigrants and the social minorities of our society. The gospel speaks to the way the economy is run and the way politics operate. The gospel of Jesus speaks not just about the world to come but how people are to live in this world that will one day be transformed by God into the new earth. *(Rev 21:1-4).*

The radical challenge of the gospel still stands but one has to ask why Christianity in our time has become so domesticated, so tame, so much a private affair between the individual and God and why it fails to stir the minds and hearts of so many young and not so young Irish Christians. Why do so many young people openly express their alienation from the Church?

PART II

A Changing Environment

CHAPTER 4

A Changing Society

Irish society has witnessed dramatic change over the past thirty years. From being largely rural and relatively stable, it has become an increasingly complex, urban society. Without their realising it, these changes have had a profound influence on people's attitude to the faith. In recent decades national priorities have changed. Gaelic or republican nationalism and Catholicism no longer have the hold they once had. The national priority now is economic growth. Rising prosperity, the politicians tell us, will produce jobs for all. What is on offer is a new vision for Ireland where happiness and success are equated with money and material possessions, with better working conditions, better pay, better housing, better holidays.

The result of such a shift in values has been that the people with real influence in Irish society are no longer teachers, bishops or priests, but those in large foreign and Irish companies, banks, insurance and commercial groups, large farmers, property owners, people in the professions, the media and skilled workers. Such people tend to see things primarily in economic terms. They judge people by what they can produce, market or sell or by what they can buy, consume or own. Those who cannot produce or sell, buy or own are relegated to the periphery of Irish society. To be 'successful' means having money and being tough, cool, hard and competitive. Power and money talk and those without either have their voices drowned out.

The stated objective of reducing unemployment has become the political slogan of the day, rather like that of restoring the language in earlier decades; no politician can afford not to make reference to it in the opening lines of a speech, though few believe it is practicable or will happen. The actual objective of the Irish, that which takes our energy and time, the one which employers and unions are prepared to regularly fight each other fiercely to achieve, and which makes high taxation the public enemy number one, is not high unemployment but money, more of it. To increase disposable income is the one goal uniting the corporate executive, trade union official, tax dodger and social welfare fraudster.

The rising graph of unemployment has been the largely irrelevant backdrop to a stage where the actors have been accountants, well-paid by managers and self-employed professional people to uncover ways of avoiding every possible penny of taxation; unions whom the increasing productivity of labour has given new leverage to extract better pay and conditions for the declining number of their members; property 'developers' and stock market 'investors' who have amassed large fortunes simply by opportunistically changing the form in which their money was held; employers who have learned how to exploit the social welfare system, temporary work schemes and so on.

Totally new ways of 'making an easy killing' have emerged as people in every rank and station of life have yielded to the pressure to increase the size of the slice of cake on their plate. For example, medical consultants employed for six months in Arab countries can earn large, tax-free salaries and invest it all in property in Spain rather than have to pay Irish tax on it when coming home; workers whose employer wants them to move to a new, modern and more comfortable plant seek large lump sums as compensation for 'disturbance'; TD's, with generous expense accounts and business interests in their home area, receive ministerial pensions along with their current TD's salary; barristers, lawyers, general practitioners, and vets find their earnings substantially increased thanks to the operation of public schemes (free legal aid, the medical card, the eradication of tuberculosis) designed to meet pressing social needs; business and training con-

33

sultants contracted by a State agency to run schemes for the unemployed are paid for one week what it will take an unemployed person on their course twenty weeks to earn; small building contractors make it a condition of employment that a job-seeker continue to draw the dole. And so on.

One could be forgiven for believing that increased prosperity is addictive to humans. Those who taste it first get hooked and single-mindedly look for more, hardening themselves to resist any threat to their rising living standards. To acknowledge continued, widespread poverty amongst the unemployed, for example, would be just such a threat.

The hardship and poverty of the unemployed in Ireland today (over 270,000 people) is not widely understood. People who grew up in the thirties and forties find it difficult to believe that financial poverty, in this age of the welfare state, can be a direct result of being on the dole. Someone unemployed can fill the empty day watching t.v. in a heated room, they point out. When they were growing up, having no job meant that you took the boat to England and its building sites or scoured around for food and fuel in fair weather and foul. The elderly, in fact, are the least complaining of all groups receiving welfare today simply because the physical hardship of their own upbringing stiffened them to withstand a lot. They grew up in an Ireland where most people supplied themselves with their own food and fuel (had a bit of land and a patch of turf), and lived in small, rural communities where a stranger was quickly spotted but – conversely – there was some sense of solidarity between families. To be poor, then, was a misfortune but did not automatically exclude a person from the community.

It is so different today. Most of our unemployed people live in urban areas where food and fuel depend on the supermarket and the ESB respectively, where social contact depends on a job and being able to go out in the evenings, where the support of relatives depends on a phone and being able to take the bus to see them. When you are reduced to living on unemployment assistance the supermarket checkout, the ESB bill, the dinner-dance ticket, the drinks round, the telephone rental, the bus tickets – all become barriers threatening to keep you out. The world will go its way, but without you. You will have no say in what you are given to live on, nor how you will get it. You will be the last to benefit when things are going well in the economy and the first to suffer when the nation goes in for belt-tightening. (The argument runs: 'If we have to close hospitals, surely we cannot afford to pay people for doing nothing' – i.e. the livelihood of unemployed people is regarded as 'money for nothing'! (cf *Unemployment: Crisis or Opportunity*. John Sweeney SJ, Centre for Faith and Justice, Dublin 1987)

The plight of the poor in Ireland tends to be ignored while middle class concerns dominate. Life has become pragmatic and competitive. Even school children get caught up in this environment through the points system as they compete with their peers for the limited number of places at university or other third level institutions. Many school leavers either emigrate, go on the dole or try to find jobs in a very limited job market. Those lucky enough to get jobs struggle to keep them or make their own way even a few steps up the promotion ladder, trying to establish themselves in an ambitiously competitive world. Competition whether for jobs, for university places or for economic security, has become an overriding preoccupation.

Young people live in a consumerist culture that throws thousands of images at them from birth; images creating envy among the poor, fostering the notion among the well-off that a happy life is defined by material possession, where the superficial becomes desirable, the desirable becomes necessary and the necessary becomes essential. Such a society is ruggedly individualistic and essentially selfish and it is here that modern society is so at odds with Christ's values. He valued compassion especially for the poor, self-giving love, hope, faith, fidelity, wonder in the face of God's creation and a deep appreciation of God's activity in the hearts of men and women: those things that make for genuine humanity. In a society where people are valued primarily in

35

economic terms, the Good News of Christ finds it difficult to make itself heard. The Good News is on the side of genuine humanity while consumerism is a call to individual isolation and to the breakdown of genuine community.

CHAPTER 5

A Privatised Religion

Irish society has fractured. Communities are fast breaking down because of emigration from rural Ireland to the cities and abroad. Our cities are no longer made up of genuine communities and people lead very isolated lives. This breakdown in community and the stress on money-making has resulted in the growth of a ruggedly competitive individualism, of a 'mé féin' mentality, which is hostile to Christian faith.

An article in the *Irish Times* throws some further light on this phenomenon. Speaking about Thatcherism and Reganism, Patrick Smyth wrote: 'The reason that increasing numbers of Americans do not vote is because they are alienated, not from the political process or politicians, but from a whole range of socially co-operative behaviour; or, in effect, from the idea of participating in social activities or society itself. The willingness of the individual to see himself as part of the collective to whom he owes responsibilities is gradually being whittled away. What appears to be happening in US society is a gradual atomisation, a breaking down of society into its constituent parts. It is bringing an increasing failure to relate to other human beings and, on a larger scale, a loss of a sense of collective identity and responsibility. Individuals are saying, like Mrs Thatcher, that "there is no such thing as society", and behaving accordingly.'

Such rugged individualism has led people to say 'My religion is my own affair and has nothing to do with anyone else. Religion is about spiritual matters and has little to do with with material and worldly problems. Oppression, a peoples' suffering, the 'dirty business of politics', are not the real concerns of religion. God is primarily concerned with my goodness or guilt and with my reward or punishment and my own goodness or guilt is a very private affair. Salvation means being saved by Jesus from my guilt and being rewarded after death in the next life where suffering and poverty have no place'.

Conventional faith is a one-to-one relationship, lived prayerfully in the depth of one's own heart. It consists of keeping the commandments, going to Mass and Confession regularly in the hope of gaining heaven in the next life. Such faith tends to be divorced from many aspects of ordinary life and people with such faith often fail to see that belief in Jesus has social as well as personal implications for what goes on in one's home, school, place of work, the sportsfield, the pub as well as in politics and the national economy. In effect conventional faith is a form of 'privatised' Christianity divorced from Monday to Saturday living. In a real sense it betrays the gospel!

Salvation has come to mean no more than 'saving one's soul' and 'the forgiveness of one's sins'. What seems to have happened is that European Christians, especially those who benefited from colonialism and were relatively well off, only felt the need to have their guilt feelings removed. They felt no need and could not imagine how anyone would feel the need to be saved from oppression, from an excess of suffering, from a system that was causing them to suffer. Such matters as these were conveniently excluded from the arena of religion and salvation by calling them 'material' and 'worldly' problems. So the gospel was taken to be concerned with only 'spiritual' matters, like the struggle with guilt and punishment for guilt. God was seen to be too pure and 'spiritual' to get involved in such ordinary matters as money or the dirty business of politics. It was very convenient for those with political power (including Churchmen for quite a long period) to see religion become a private matter between God and the individual soul. The individual Christian who was 'saved' from guilt by Jesus would be rewarded after death in that other world where there are no material problems like suffering or poverty and these could then be conveniently ignored and glossed over in this world.

But Salvation in the Bible is salvation from all sorts of suffering, not simply personal guilt. The Jewish people, for example, were saved from real slavery in Egypt. Wherever people suffer, either individually or collectively, there is need for salvation not just in the next world but in this one as well. Because most people in Ireland over the past thirty years may not have experienced oppression or exploitation, they may not have felt the need for corporate solidarity as their forefathers did in the centuries of persecution. But those who do suffer exploitation, the poor, the lonely, the unemployed, the handicapped, those forced to emigrate, do realise their need of salvation from their suffering.

Just as Christ spent his time alleviating suffering in all its forms by meeting the real needs of real people, so today the mission of his Church is to carry on the same task. In Christ's words, the task of the Christian community is to feed the hungry, receive the stranger, clothe the naked, visit the sick and prisoners, to serve the least important in human eyes, and so to serve God himself. Christianity is not merely, and sometimes selfishly, a matter of 'saving one's own soul'.

One cannot underestimate the challenges to Christianity that have come from a flawed interpretation of Christ's message, the breakdown in community and the transformation in Irish life styles and expectations. The arrival of a full-blown consumerist society in Ireland has presented a challenge to the Church which she has had difficulty facing up to. Church leaders, parents and educators may bemoan the loss of Church-going among young people but perhaps their analysis of the problem has been too glib and underestimated the forces that are at work. Indeed the Church itself may have become part of the problem!

Many young people regard the Church rather like a large multi-national corporation with impersonal orders issuing from head-quarters in Rome or the branch office of the local Bishop. They do not feel involved but rather preached at. Women, in particular, are often resentful at their exclusion from any real say in the Church's affairs and are deeply hurt at the lack of consultation about such intimate matters as their sexuality. Young people find Mass 'boring' and the language of the Church incomprehensible.

To understand the Church, one has to begin with a fact that may surprise some Catholics. While the message of Christ is offered to the whole world, at no time in history has every human being ever been a member of the Church nor is there any reason to believe that this will be the case in the future. Yet the Church claims to be universal (Catholic) and indeed this is so in the sense that no human being or human even lies outside its concerns. Yet while its message is for all men and women, only some will actually be called to join it.

There seems to be two parts to God's plan for the world: one part relating to all men and women; the other only to those whom God calls in a special way to be members of the Church. These two aspects of God's intentions have profound implications for all those concerned with young people and their faith.

All human beings are created by God and have been endowed with Divine Power, by which I mean the potential of living lives of self-giving love. They are created in the image of a triune God who is a Love Event. The ability to give oneself in love to others comes from God and is offered to all men and women. 'God is Love, and whoever lives in love lives in union with God and God lives in union with him(or her),' as St John put it. The ultimate destiny of human beings is to be united with one another in the Love Event that is God.

But while everyone may be endowed with this potential for self-giving love, this is not the way many choose to live their lives. People are profoundly influenced by their social environment and today society socialises them into the values of competitive individualism, consumerism, selfishness, possessiveness and money as the measure of all value. Modern society encourages people to see themselves as having a right to total freedom in all things where the first and only duty is to oneself. In such a society self-giving love is devalued because it always involves a struggle to go beyond one's own selfish interests and look to the well-being of others.

The second stage in God's plan for the world is the birth of an community, the body of Christ, the People of God, the Church. God sent Jesus into the world to rekindle in the hearts of men and women the desire for self-giving love which is the only thing that will redeem humanity from all that dehumanises it. Jesus gathered about him a band of followers, an assembly, a Church, a community of those who were to follow him in life and death: a community who would strive, however inadequately, to live as he lived and, if necessary, to die as he died in the cause of justice, truth, freedom and love. It is within this community, whatever its human limitations, that God has chosen to reveal himself and his plans for humanity down the ages. Jesus revealed to his followers the Good News that all human beings, especially the poorest and weakest and most despised, are sons and daughters of a common Father and are destined for unity in love with one another and with God in a new heaven and a new earth that is being created now throughout history. The birth, life, death and resurrection of Jesus took place to make this plan known and to help make it a reality in the world. The task of the Church, its mission, is to continue Jesus' work as a community of believers: to be a light in the darkness of the world. Christians are those who know what God is striving to achieve and try to live lives of self-forgetful love so that they may assist in the great vocation of bringing justice and love, unity and peace into God's world (or building up the Kingdom, to use religious language).

Consequently, the Church does not exist for itself. It exists to be a sign for those outside the Church. Like Jesus, it is in the world not to be served but to serve by striving to bring about a union of minds and hearts among all peoples. Jesus' prayer was 'may they be one, as you Father are in me and I in you are one.'

The fact that some people decide not to become members of such a Church or are not called to be members of it, does not mean that

41

they are 'lost' to God. All who try to live lives of love for others will find God and become one with him. This should be a source of consolation to those who grieve that their sons or daughters have ceased to be 'practising' Christians in the accepted sense.

But the Church, the community of believers, is also a community of sinners. Within the hearts and minds of its members the struggle between the life-giving forces of love and the death-giving forces of selfishness continues. As a member of the Church, the battle between egotism and selflessness goes on in my heart and in the hearts and minds of all Christians just as it went on in the hearts and minds of Jesus' disciples who fought about having the highest places in the Kingdom or whether new members should be circumcised or not. Not all was peace and light in those adolescent days of the Christian Church! Yet, as St Paul put it, 'God chose what is foolish by human reckoning to shame the strong'. Christ came to call sinners and still does so, even within a sinful Church.

The sinfulness of the Church, however, prevents many young people from being able to respond adequately to the call of Christ. This sinfulness is bound up with its history, with its failures as a genuine community and with the 'privatisation' of Christ's message.

CHAPTER 6

The Church as Institution

A major obstacle to faith among young people is their experience of the Church as institution. The Church as we know it today has evolved over many centuries. Many of its present structures originated centuries ago with the birth of Christendom in Europe. This alliance of Church and State took place in a period before people thought of themselves in the individual ways they do now. The individual was seen primarily as belonging to a tribe or a family. This 'belonging' meant strict control of tribe members which offered security in the face of other hostile tribes or the natural world. Such strict control over time set down firm roots. The tribe transmitted traditional values, norms and skills which, over a relatively stable period of history, enabled it to confront all the foreseeable challenges of life. The tribe, family or clan also threw up a class system which was seen as inevitable as the laws of nature. Since the various tribes tended to be isolated from one another, the individual became dependent on his or her tribe and was controlled by it. While individual liberty was restricted, there was a feeling of security because the group reduced unpredictability to the maximum.

It was within this sort of society that the Church became institutionalised. In the face of a hostile world, the Church had to confront the problems of unity and survival after Christ disappeared. Church membership grew rapidly and so the institutional side of church life had to be bolstered both to organise the growing number of converts as well as control them. While at the time this was quite laudable, a number of factors tended to militate against the deeper aspects of Christ's message. New members entered the

Church by birth and this was not necessarily followed later by a personal conversion to the attitudes and mindset of Christ. The summons to conversion was replaced by a hereditary faith and this faith was to be 'handed on' from one generation to the next. In the relatively stable societies that existed up to recent times the main task of the Church came to be seen as preserving and handing on the faith. Church membership was a matter of routine.

Christendom coincided with the Roman Empire and, for political reasons, the Emperors required oneness of faith to provide political stability to the empire. Down the centuries religion has played a very important part in providing meaning to society, but it has also been used to maintain the status quo even where a particular regime was oppressive. Leaders could and did argue that poverty and suffering had to be accepted because they were God's will but that the oppressed would gain their reward in the next life. 'Pie in the sky when you die' was not invented by Karl Marx!

Within Christendom, the universality of the Church came to be seen in quantative terms: getting as many people as possible into the Church so that they could be saved. In such an atmosphere the missionary activity of the Church ceased to be seen as a task for every Christian and became the work of specialists directed towards the pagan world. It was assumed that in Europe there were no pagans, only good or bad Christians. Missionary activity even took it for granted that Christianising and Westernising were one and the same.

When the Church hierarchy assumed political power in later generation, it assumed all the traditional trappings that went with it. The Church was transformed into a 'Christian Society' with a well-built ideology that defended the establishment, for now it was that establishment. Church authority came to be seen in secular terms as authority to command and expect obedience. Prince-Bishops and Popes were heads of state and commanders of armies as well as leaders of Christ's Church.

Some of the tensions in the Church today reflect those elements of

Christendom that still persist in its structures and are very much at odds with the prevailing culture of participative democracy. What is at stake here is power and the way power is exercised. Central to the Gospel is the question of power. Christ came to bring salvation to the world: salvation from sin, from personal guilt on the one hand but salvation from all forms of suffering whether personal or corporate on the other. Salvation involves the use of power. It is about the struggle for power; the power of God on the one hand or the power of evil men on the other.

It is those with power who control the lives of those who suffer and so it is important to understand power; to know who has it and how it is maintained; to know who or what is a threat to that power and how the threat is being contained. It is important to discover the forces for change in society and see which of them are likely to cause injustice and which could lead towards justice. Sin and salvation are fundamentally questions about power.

Power has been defined as 'the basic energy to initiate and sustain action, translating intention into reality'. In the course of history, power has implied insensitivity, cruelty and corruption. Power, however, is both necessary for action and, at the same time, is very much distrusted. People experience power all the time from birth to death. 'It is implicit in every human interaction – familial, sexual, occupational, national and international – either covertly or overtly. Throughout history, leaders have controlled rather than organised, administered repression rather than expression, and held their followers in arrestment rather than in evolution.' (Cf *Leaders*, Warren Bernis and Burt Manus. Harper and Row, New York 1985)

As a Headmaster for some fifteen years, I have known power, albeit of a limited nature. I have had the power to initiate new plans or to stop those of others from being implemented. I have had the power to hire or make life difficult for those in my employment. I have had the power to control and administer my own plans rather than let others share in my power. I have had the power to command obedience of pupils and staff, rather than facilitate co-operation and growth in building up the school community. Power can be an awesome thing. Oppressive regimes, military, political, economic or technological can wield awesome power over the hearts, minds and bodies of millions and are open to colossal abuse. While all power comes ultimately from God, the abuse of power is the result of selfishness and greed.

God's 'power' is of a different order. Service is the key. God's power is the power of service. Jesus put it this way: 'You know that the men who are considered rulers of the heathen have power over them and the leaders have complete authority. This, however, is not to be the way it is among you. If one of you wants to be great, he must be the servant of the rest; and if one of you wants to be first, he must be the slave of all. For even the Son of Man did not come to be served; he came to serve and to give his life to redeem many people'. (*Mt 20:26-28*). Authority is usually taken to mean the power to command others and to be able to enforce those commands; to lay down the law and expect to have it obeyed. The authority of Christ, on the other hand, is the power to care for others, to wash their feet, to look to their interests, to serve their deepest needs, to be the slave of all, not to lord it over people and make one's authority felt.

Here we touch on one of the factors that alienate young people from the Church. Power in the Church is perceived in the same way as secular power. Bishops and priests assumed the authority to command others and expected those commands to be obeyed. However, authority and the use of power is no longer accepted unquestioningly in either State or Church. Today's generation is only too keenly aware of the abuse of power from Stalin and Hitler to Saddam Hussein not to be wary of it. When the Church adopts a secular mode of authority instead of that advocated by Jesus, it too is suspect in our time. The power of the Church, as it was for Christ, must be the power of service. The Church's mission is to invite people to share Christ's vision and to build the faithful into Christian communities that will be a source of light and service to the world. St Peter in his first letter sets the tone for

Church leaders. 'I am a witness of Christ's sufferings, and I will share in the glory that will be revealed. I appeal to you to be shepherds of the flock that God gave you and to take care of it willingly, as God wants you to, and not unwillingly. Do you work, not for mere pay, but from a real desire to serve. Do not try to rule over those who have been put in your care, but be an example of the flock.' (5:1-4)

As a Headmaster, I was well aware that it was a pointless task to 'issue orders from above' if one wanted to bring unity and purpose to a school. Orders from above produce alienation. People need to be involved and share in the decision-making process. But when there is very little involvement of lay Catholics in the process of discerning what the gospel means in their lives: where they do not have a part in the actual decision-making process; where there is no sense of building a community with a sense of mission together, then both pastors and people fail to become a real Church. Above all, where the poorest and weakest members of the church do not feel involved in its decision making processes then they too fail to have that sense of dignity that should come from being brothers and sisters in Christ even though, as Jesus said, the Kingdom belongs to them.

Seen from the world's usual perspective, God's power of service seems like weakness. St Paul expressed it in these terms: 'The language of the cross may be illogical to those who are not on the way to salvation, but those of us who are on the way see it as God's power to save'. (1 Cor 1:18). The language of the cross is the language of one who was prepared to die in the cause of truth, justice and love. But the powerful seemed to win. Christ's mission seemed a failure and yet it resulted in victory because it drew people to him (Jn 12:23) and led to the creation of new people, 'Christ's body' (Eph 1:23) of which Christians are members (Eph 5:30); a body that was to be filled with and live by his Spirit (Acts 2:1-13) and be a light to the world down the centuries. This body was to be a new community called Church.

47

CHAPTER 7

The Church as Community

The Church claims to be the Body of Christ and calls itself the Christian Community. However one must ask whether in Ireland today it possesses the characteristics of a genuine community? Are parishes, for example, communities where people are really committed to serving the needs of the poor and those on the margins of our society? Are parishioners free to speak their minds and, with their clergy, try to arrive at a consensus as to what the parish should be doing to spread the Good News of Christ? Do parishioners share their joys and sorrows or do they live in isolation, making their lonely way to God? Do they find healing and acceptance in the community or does reconciliation simply mean personal forgiveness in the confessional? Do Church members have a sense of common purpose and mission, not only to themselves but to a suffering world? To answer these questions one must look for the characteristics of a genuine community.

Genuine communities are made up of people who are committed to one another in some way, share a common vision or goal. They have a sense of purpose that gives coherence and meaning to what they are doing together. They have a mission. Such a mission can be the scratching out of an existence for themselves and their families in the realisation that only through common effort will they be able to survive. The mission can be that of an environmental group trying to save the planet from destruction, or communities like those formed by Jean Vanier trying to bring love and acceptance into the lives of the handicapped.

A common factor in genuine communities is that its members, in pursuing their vision, are prepared to communicate honestly with one other. Such honest communication does not come easily; it is a hard and painful process. But without it a community is such only in name. To achieve such communication means giving time, effort and commitment to others, which people may not be willing to do out of fear or apathy. Commitment of people to one another is the crucial factor in building community. There may be differences of personality, education, and ability in any community but it learns to transcend such individual differences by making the time and giving the commitment to doing so. Differences are overcome not by voting or by a leader taking all the decisions but by people arriving at a consensus so that everyone is involved in the decision-making process and all take part together in striving for the common goal.

In a genuine community individuals can speak their minds and even go against the trend. The resulting consensus, born of many differing viewpoints, is more effective than decision-making by one or two people because a wider view of any problems is gained than can be achieved by the few.

When people work together as a community, they tend to grow in realism and humility. When I experience the talents and limitations, the joys and sorrows of other people's lives I see my own life in a truer perspective. Individualism is often arrogant but when I appreciate other people's gifts or brokenness, I become aware of my own gifts and brokenness and my arrogance is diminished.

A genuine community is a healing community where old wounds are healed, old resentments are forgotten, old resistance overcome, though not without serious effort. The extraordinary thing is that where genuine community is fostered, where people communicate in some depth, healing and conversion happen not because people try to convert or heal one another but, because in accepting others as they are, they are able to heal themselves. Acceptance by others is like good soil that permits wheat to grow and develop to the full. Acceptance enables me to become my true self: it releases in me a capacity to grow and that capacity is entirely within myself planted there by God. If a community provides the

49

soil of acceptance it enables me to realise my humanity more fully; to accept both my talents and my limitations, my joys as well as my sorrows. I am free to be me and I can discard my defenses, my masks, my disguises: free to seek my own psychological and spiritual health, because, above all, the community provides me with the inner feeling of being loved. To be accepted as I am is truly an act of love because to feel accepted is to feel loved.

Finally a real community is one that examines itself regularly as to the quality of its own relationships and is aware of what is going on both within the community itself and in the world outside. Any community that fails to take account of what is happening beyond its borders will soon become self preoccupied and selfish.

The western world has lost this sense of community and individualism has taken its place. Because Irish society has atomised, the conditions needed for genuine communities have also disappeared. Perhaps this is why so many young people drift to various sects or other groups that give them a feeling of belonging which the Church fails to provide.

The Church is meant to be a closely united group of people with a sense of mission. Christ used the analogy of the vine and its branches. St Paul spoke of the Body of Christ. 'All of you are Christ's body, and each one is a part of it', he wrote to the Corinthians. The Church's mission is to be a genuine community that bring Good News to the poor and responds to real human needs as Jesus did: in simplicity, in honesty, in truth and most of all in love. Its mission is the salvation of the world no less: salvation from sin; from all that causes suffering, corporate as well as personal. Its mission is to bring all peoples into unity so that they may be one as Christ and the Father are one, in love. The Church and each of its constituent communities exists not for its own satisfaction but to carry out that mission of bringing into existence the Kingdom (or Reign of God) by preaching, practising and if necessary dying for the Good News of the brother/sisterhood of humanity under the Fatherhood of God.

Jesus said 'If there is love among you, then will you be my disciples,' (*Jn 13:35*). Self-giving love forms the Christian community and binds it together but love calls for mutual sharing and giving: a sharing of what one is and has with those in need; a sharing of faith and hope. A Christian community is a community of mutual help in which people practice real encounter and fraternal love not simply by reading or thinking about it but by offering real, concrete help to one another so as to more effectively serve those in need in society. It is also a community that can expect resistance and persecution for it is at odds with the prevailing selfishness and greed of contemporary society.

A Christian community is also a discerning, reflective community. In other words, it gives space in our noise-polluted world to create an inward stillness so that its members can take their search for God and his will for the world seriously in a spirit of prayer. Prayer means more than 'saying prayers'. To pray is to realise that the God of Love is active within the community and in each of its members. 'Where two or three are gathered in my name, I am there in the midst of them', Jesus said. (*Mt 16:20*) From the realisation of Christ's activity in each and every man and woman, myself included, comes the ability to love others from a deeper part of oneself. A Christian community is one that reflects on the gospel together, seeks out its significance for life today as it strives to help meet the needs of those who suffer.

When people come together to carry on Christ's work of bringing Good News to the poor, of proclaiming liberty to captives, of setting the oppressed free, then Jesus is alive and present in the world. He is present in his Body, a Church filled and alive with his Spirit. To be honestly and truly gathered in his name means that people search together for ways of genuinely and honestly responding to the human needs of the world as Christ did. When Jesus met a blind man, a leper or a widow and her dead son, he responded in love to this situation. He did what he could with no hooks attached. He responded in a very human way to a human need. A Christian community does the same. It is not just a question of 'doing one's Christian duty or gathering as isolated individuals to 'receive the sacraments' but, gathered in his name, the community strives to emulate Jesus in finding ways of praising God for his creation and of responding to the actual needs of the human community both personal and social.

CHAPTER 8

Sacraments that Make Sense

When people are praying together, struggling together for the same ideals and shouldering the burden of Christian sacrifice, then Church and Sacraments take on a new and vital meaning. A Christian on her own finds it difficult to celebrate the Good News or to deal with the human needs of others. Poverty, hunger, unemployment, bureaucratic indifference to the needs of the physically or mentally handicapped, or the abuse of human rights, can be daunting challenges for any one individual. A Christian community, on the other hand, is in a far stronger position to speak out of a deep faith and try to put right those things that dehumanise. It can witness to the Good News with more authenticity and more authority. In the process, its sacramental life also begins to take on new meaning.

One of the reasons why sacraments 'don't work' for young people is that their communitarian dimension has been lost. They have been 'privatised'. Traditional Catholics tend to see the sacraments in almost semi-magical terms, as a sort of direct link to God. For them the sacraments do not seem to have much to do with earning one's living, paying the mortgage, changing nappies, preparing meals, doing a day's work in an office, factory or school, being on the dole, having to emigrate or fighting for justice. Still less do they seem to have anything to do with politics or economics. They are seen not as activities pertaining to a whole community but almost as magical rites that link the individual to God in some mysterious way.

The sacred and secular have, for historical reasons, become separated. The sacred or spiritual is seen to be 'above' and 'beyond' the ordinary affairs of life. Jesus, on the other hand, said that God is to be found not in some world 'above' but in the concrete reality of daily relationships and that these relationships even take precedence over strictly religious matters. 'So if you are about to offer your gift to God at the altar and there you remember that your brother has something against you, leave your gift there in front of the altar, go at once and make peace with your brother, and then come back and offer your gift to God.' *(Mt 5:23)*. God is not to be found 'beyond the clouds'. The real miracle is that when one senses the beauty of nature, eats a hearty meal, makes love, dances, smells lilac in the spring, feeds the hungry, receives the stranger, takes care of the sick, visits the prisoner, one finds God. The tendency all the time is to move from the human to a different, more sacred level: to try to find God above the messy situations of human existence and try to placate or manipulate him with prayers or sacred rites.

Prayer is a good example of this. People approach prayer very differently when they realise that they meet God in the many opportunities of daily living where they have to choose for or against love, for or against other human beings. How parents deal with their children, teachers with their pupils, employers with their employees, the rich with the poor, rich nations with poor ones, determine how they deal with God who lives in all human beings giving them life, growth, feeling and intelligence. On the other hand, people who identify daily life with the profane and see prayer only as a time to restore calm to the spirit in a separate realm of the sacred are moving away from Jesus' way of looking at the world. Prayer for Jesus was a way of communing with God so as to discover God's will and it always led him back to this world and especially to those in need.

Many older Christians are content with a direct link to God, as it were, in the depth of their own hearts. A younger generation finds this 'otherworldly' approach unsatisfying as it seems to have so little to do with the challenges of ordinary life. Hence young people find the Mass boring. They have stopped going to Confession. They are alienated from religious practice because they refuse to be alienated from life and, in a profound sense, they are right because the Good News of Jesus is about life on earth, not simply in the hereafter. In the Our Father one prays 'Thy Kingdom come' and, what amounts to the same thing, 'Thy will be done on earth.' The Church has to stop separating the physical or the natural or the human from the spiritual and cease concentrating only on the spiritual. This was not the way of Christ. A Christian community, like Jesus, begins with a human response to human needs, informed by the spirit of Love. Evangelisation is not the preaching of some disincarnate spirituality but, as it was for Jesus, the expression of love for men and women and the world in which they live.

If young people were invited to join genuinely reflectively, discerning communities that tried to find God in all things human, that set out to meet human needs and alleviate suffering, they might find that the sacraments were no longer 'boring'.

For any Christian community there are key moments in its existence in which life-giving as well as life-denying forces gather together and become tangible. When, for example, grave injustice is being done to the starving, the poor, the young, women, minorities, the old or the sick, life-denying forces are at work. When human beings become expandable for a political cause death-bearing forces are at work. When, on the other hand, the community celebrates moments of birth, life-giving forces are at work. These key moments of life are celebrated by the Christian community in those signs called Sacraments. Sacraments are signs for the community, not just for individuals. They highlight how God is at work in the community preparing it for and assisting it in its mission. Just as families celebrate birthdays every year, so the Christian community celebrates important moments in its own life. Let us look at some of these key moments and their significance in a genuinely Christian community.

Baptism

Many parents are concerned that young people do not always bother to have their children baptised. The real problem, however, has to do with the coherence and meaningfulness of the Christian community as such. The 'privatisation' of faith has downplayed the importance of community and so people fail to see that Baptism, like all the other Sacraments, is basically a community activity and only has meaning for the community. Baptism is a sign for the community which indicates the action of God in its life. Where Christians fail to form genuine communities this sign function may lose all meaning.

A new born baby is fragile and defenceless. It needs a community to save it from death. In the first instance that community is the family into which it is born. However many questions arise in western society that need to be faced. Society may not want this child. It may prove an incumberance to one's standard of living or get in the way of one's enjoyment of life. Children born into the world of the poor are often seen in western eyes as a threat because people prefer to preserve their standards of living or explore outer space rather than put their resources at the disposal of the children of the poor.

Even if the newborn child survives rejection, it has to gradually find its way in society. 'Society' is a given, something we benefit from or suffer under. It is the social climate into which we are born and which affects us from birth. It includes our language, our social customs, our political and economic structures as well as our in-built attitudes to family, to work, to property and possessions, to authority, to other classes and to the state. It is an ethos that we absorb and which affects us from the day we are born. As we grow up we are socialised into its values and into its ways of looking at the world. Today a child may well grow up to be egotistical and hard nosed as it absorbs the false values of individualism, selfishness, competitiveness, and money as the measure of everything. This is original sin that we inherit; the system of false values we are born into and from which we need to be saved if we are to live life to the full.

A Christian community, realising that a child is born into a sinful world, also knows that as a community it is enriched by a love that has its source in God. In Baptism it undertakes to share and nurture that love as it welcomes the newborn into the Christian family. It commits itself to nurturing the child's human growth in the fullest sense of the word in spite of all those forces at work in the world that will oppose it. The community commits itself to opposing such evils for it 'renounces Satan and all his works'.

People left to themselves tend to be apathetic, to do the minimum that is required to survive without having to face the challenges of life. Life is difficult, a matter of constantly meeting and solving problems and when people refuse to face up to their problems they encounter grief, frustration, guilt, sadness, loneliness, despair, anxiety and fear. Rather than facing their problems, they pretend they do not exist, put off doing anything about them, ignore them, hope that they will go away or take to drink or drugs to help forget about them. Apathy exists in every one of us: infants, children, adolescents, adults, the elderly, the wise, the stupid, the lame and the whole. It is at work holding back our human growth which always cries out for nurture. A Christian community, on the other hand, can provide that nurture for it knows that such apathy can be overcome, that there is another, opposing source of power available to it, the power of Grace. Grace is a great God-given inner and personalising force coming from outside ourselves that effectively and unconsciously enables us to overcome human apathy and all other barriers to human growth by prompting and urging us forward towards the fullness of our humanity. When we experience compassion or courage and strength to bear the unbearable, or faith and hope in facing the challenge to human growth, we experience Grace at work. A Christian community at the moment of Baptism accepts that such power is given to it and promises to nourish it in the heart and mind of the new member of the community.

There is no inherent sinfulness in newborn infants, no 'black marks on the soul' as it were. Rather they are born into an apathetic and sinful world. In the sacrament of Baptism the symbolism makes the community aware of the graceful power of life and the potential for human growth which is a God-given gift to all of us. At the same time the powers of evil and of sin, social as well as personal, from which the community needs to be washed clean are indicated. Baptism makes the community aware of the forces for good and evil that will affect the life of the new born child (or the adult receiving baptism) and commits itself to nurturing human growth in the life of the newly baptised Christian. Baptism can come alive when it is seen as a community activity: a sign of initiation into a community, the body of Christ, committed to spreading the Good News of Jesus.

Confirmation
Comments by some Sixth Year Students:
'A day when you are supposed to feel a spiritual movement, but really it's just a day off school where you dress up and get money from your relatives.' 'Confirmation means very little to me.' 'About £150 and a pat on the back from the neighbours.' 'I think children are too young making their Confirmation to understand any spiritual meaning it should have. The ordeal is a happy day in their lives in which they receive lots of presents and money. I don't find it very convincing. However I don't think about Confirmation a lot because I don't understand it.'

As a young person starts to discover freedom, a moment comes when the Christian community has to ask whether that liberty will be able to survive the many challenges that now confronts it. Will the young person be able to live according to Christ's values, especially with regard to the poor and suffering of the world? Can this young person face up to the rugged individualism, selfishness and greed of society and be an active member of the community in bringing the Good News of Christ to the world? When the Bishop, representing the Christian community, lays his hands on and anoints the young person, he is signifying that the young person has come of age and now, as a full-blown member of the community, is mature enough and strong enough to make the faith his own and take part in its mission. By anointing the young person the community signifies that, through the power of the Spirit, it will provide the strength to help the young person overcome the obstacles to human growth that lie in the way so that she may be better able to take a fruitful part in the mission of Christ.

This will happen, in the first instance, if the community is serious in its efforts to incorporate the young person into a genuine community by way of love and acceptance which have to be demonstrated if they are to be effective. If the Christian community is unwilling to listen and to talk constructively to young people, they will not be prepared to become part of that community which, in the sacrament of Confirmation, undertakes to confirm its members in the gifts of the Spirit that enables them to bring Good News to the world.

The sacrament of Confirmation is in crisis precisely because it has lost this communitarian dimension. For many young people it is a meaningless sacrament. The Church talks about the giving of the gifts of the Spirit but such gifts are given to enable solidarity, communion and mutual help in the Christian mission. The real moment of Confirmation is when a young person who is old enough agrees to play a full part in the life and mission of the Christian Community and draws his or her strength from that community gathered in Christ's name. It should be a solemnly marked initiation ceremony, in the Spirit, into adult participation in the mission of Christ.

The Eucharist
Some comments by sixth year students:
'I've given up going to Mass. To me it's boring.' 'I go when I feel like going.' 'I find it silly when people call themselves Catholics when all they do is go to Mass.' 'I don't go but when I do its only to keep my parents happy on special occasions.'

The first Christian communities lived in an environment with an imposing array of religious rituals but the strange thing was that they had no sacred rites of their own in the strict sense. They did not have a temple but met in family houses. They assembled for 'thanks giving' and 'breaking bread'. They did not offer sacrifices to the gods as the pagans did. What came first was a community, the community called the ecclesia, the gathering, the Church and this community developed signs and gestures that signified the activity of God in its life. Christian liturgy grew out of community living as people took on board the life, death and resurrection of Jesus and asked themselves what significance it had for their activity here and now.

There is always a danger, however, that Christians in order to make their message 'relevant' will adapt their liturgy to the prevailing culture. The early Christians, who did not want to be accused of being atheists since they did not offer sacrifices, began to speak of what Jesus had initiated as 'gesture' and 'sign' as 'sacrifice' and 'offering'. They adapted their way of talking about what they were doing so as to make it relevant to those outside the community. But for some Christians 'sacrifice' soon took on the pagan connotation of a sacred act endowed with some peculiar power of its own and so they came to talk about 'Eucharist Sacrifice' or the 'Sacrifice of the Mass'. The idea of Christ having to die to placate an angry Father took hold in the minds of many Christians. This was a betrayal of Jesus' *Abba* and a return to a pagan understanding of the relationship between human beings and God. It was a separation of the sacred and the human that Christ had tried to overcome because any such separation soon degenerates into magic.

There is no doubt that Jesus did offer his life in sacrifice. Indeed real sacrifice is what is required in every truly human act: self-sacrifice, self-giving that is part of all true love. Such sacrifice is not something mystical but something reasonable and ordinary. Jesus did not give his life to placate an angry God but as an act of self-giving love out of compassion for and solidarity with those who suffered. Jesus was put to death because he challenged those responsible for the oppression and suffering of his people. Because he showed the poor and broken how to attain true inner freedom through love and compassion, he undermined the powerful and they had him put to death. He died not to placate his Father but out of love for his father's children. He did not want to die but if he could draw people to himself and to his vision of what the world could be then he was prepared to make the supreme sacrifice out of love. Christ died because evil men could not tolerate the light of what he had to say but his death cast even greater light on the human situation so that generation after generation was drawn to him. God, like a father seeing his son fight for justice in an oppressive situation, realised that Jesus would die for his efforts but because of his compassion for our human plight and for the eventual freedom that Christ's life and death would bring to many, broken-heartedly accepted his son's sacrifice.

Whenever people try to promote justice, truth and love they evoke resistance from those with their own interests to preserve. The powerful do not want people to question the corrupt system that gives them power or privilege. When Jesus was led to the place of execution he accepted this fundamental law. He was aware of it and did not dodge it. To bring his work to completion, he chose to accept that every positive effort on behalf of justice for the poor or the oppressed encounters violent resistance. The more profound and decisive the required work of transformation that someone tries to bring about in society the more violent the resistance will be. Understood in this sense, sacrifice ceases to be something occult or magic. On the contrary, it is the act of a human being fully exercising his or her freedom on behalf of others.

This is the sacrifice that Jesus made and it is the same sacrifice which unties the Christian community in its struggles with all forms of evil. Jesus is present through the words, signs and gestures of the liturgy reminding us of his sacrifice ('This is my body which is given for you'), and inviting us, as his body present in the world today, to sacrifice ourselves for others in the same way. ('Do this in memory of me'). Jesus' self-sacrifice seals the new pact, the new covenant, between God and humanity. The self-sacrifice of Christ on behalf of his beloved poor and suffering people and its acceptance by the Father is to be continued in his body, the Church. It too is to wash the feet of those who suffer. Such sacrifice will entail moments of suffering, hardship and hate. 'If the world hates you, you must remember that it has hated me first'. But such sacrifice will also entail moments of celebration and thanks-giving to God for his presence among his people and his activity in their lives. All of these are essential ingredients of the eucharist celebration.

The early Christians saw their religion as essentially different from that of others and they dispensed with temples, altars and sacrifices. Instead they became the temple, the living temple of God. Jesus took the old ideas of priesthood and sacrifice and gave them a totally new meaning. St Peter spelt this out in his first letter: 'But you are a chosen race, a royal priesthood, a consecrated nation, a people set apart to sing the praises of God who called you out of darkness into his wonderful light. Once you were not a people at all, and now you are the people of God'. *(2:9)* The Christian community, as such, is priestly; it sacrifices itself to God in union with the self-sacrifice of Christ and the privileged moment of this celebration is in the Eucharist.

A mere congregation of people hardly constitutes a community in any real sense. Merely listening to liturgical readings and to a sermon every Sunday hardly enables people to grasp the full significance of the gospel in their lives and become a self-sacrificing community of service, a priestly people or a 'light to the world'. But once one begins to see the Eucharist as the celebration of a community which unites itself to the self-offering of Christ and which draws nourishment from its union with him, then it is seen in a very different way from the private devotion that is a common perception among Christians. The community called Church is the body of Christ, the dwelling place of God's Spirit, responding as Christ did to those who are in agony. His Body, the Church are the men and women who strive to alleviate that suffering, who respond to ordinary human needs in a very human way and in this way carry on the mission of Christ.

If the Eucharist is to be of significance in young peoples' lives this sense of a community searching together to love and serve God by loving and serving the real needs of those who suffer in society has to be rediscovered. Church-going may be 'boring' because its ceremonies do not reflect any depth of mutual commitment and action on behalf of God's poor but merely signify a coexistence that caricatures love.

All Sacraments are signs dealing with moments in the life of the community when life-giving or death-bearing forces are at work. But, as signs, they presume Faith and a few words on faith may be in order at this point. To build a genuine community demands a deep and conscious faith. St Luke recounts the story of the Roman officer who had a servant who was very dear to him. This servant was sick and about to die. When the officer heard about Jesus, he sent some Jewish elders to entreat Jesus to heal his servant. The officer was a foreigner, a member of the Roman occupying force and yet here was a man of whom Jesus said 'I tell you, not even in Israel have I found faith like this.' Clearly Jesus was not speaking about the officer's faith in dogmas or doctrines but his belief that Jesus could cure his servant. He believed that Jesus had the power to overcome the evil that was sickness with the good that is health. Jesus responded to this very human need.

To believe that evil will in the end always be conquered by goodness is what separates people of faith from those who have none. To really believe that God is at work in the world and that all evil can be overcome in spite of sickness, tragedy, war, famine, disease and death, is to have faith.

Such faith is never easy for all the evidence seems to go against it. The wicked prosper, injustice and hate prevail, sickness and disease are everyday occurrences, family tragedies all to frequent. Yet faith tells us that, in spite of all, the goodness of God will overcome all such evil and not just in the next life. It is hard to believe that in spite of a son's cancer, the death of a loved one, the tragedy that has left a daughter paralysed, the starvation of millions in Africa, nonetheless goodness will win out. Just as the men of evil seemed to conquer Christ and had him killed on a cross, so evil in all its many guises seems to win out in people's lives.

Real faith is something deep; deeper than any tragedy that can befall human beings. Such faith, where it is nurtured, can take them deep into themselves as individuals or as communities, beyond pain and tragedy to find God as Jesus did in his last agony when he said 'into your hands I commend my spirit'. It is no easy journey and to pretend otherwise is to belittle faith.

Such faith is a gift of God but it *is* a gift; that is to say it is given to me and, like the powers of intellect or reason, it is something I have to develop and encourage to grow. Initially it is like a mustard seed, but it can become a powerful force in my life. Jesus, in speaking of faith, used phrases like 'your faith has saved you'; 'your faith has restored you to health'. Deep faith in God and in others can move mountains: it is a powerful force because if I believe that God is a God of compassion and love, then, through faith, I can unleash these two great forces into my life. I can, as it were, tune into God and he can use me as an instrument of his love and peace, often in ways known only to himself. While this is true for the individual, it is even more significant for a Christian community as it faces the insidious challenges of evil and suffering. The many martyrs of communism or the Jesuits murdered in El Salvador bear witness to this.

If anything can save our world from destruction it is compassion and self-giving and it is faith that brings these into play. The Roman officer, though a foreigner as far as the chosen people were concerned, drew the admiration of Jesus because of the compassion and self-forgetful love he had for his servant and for the trust he had in Christ's power to save him.

Such faith is called for when any community has to face sickness or death or injustice of any sort. Even when the community has to resign itself to being passive in the face of the many evils in the world, they can become active instruments of love for they point towards Resurrection either beyond this life or as signs of hope in the battle against evil in the here and now. Christ died for human-kind and the Body of Christ was born. Many died to fight the evils of Nazism or Communist dictatorships and democracy and free-dom were won as a result of their resolve and fortitude as they helped build the new earth.

Faith is born in prayer and meditation, communal as well as per-sonal. Indeed a community that does not pray together does not stay together. We priests have, in many ways, let down our fellow Christians by not opening up to them the inherited riches of Christian prayer. The crisis of faith in our time can be attributed in part to a lack of prayer in people's lives. Just as the married couple that do not communicate drift apart, so the Christian community that does not pray together falls apart.

Each Christian community is given the liberating message that the father of love and compassion is active in its midst; that all men and women are sons and daughters of a loving Father and as such possess a great dignity. If the community is to receive and share this Good News it needs signs and symbols to make itself conscious of the gracious love of God. Human beings need signs and symbols to communicate effectively; a word, a handshake, an embrace, a kiss, a celebration. The Church's sacramental signs are meant to make clear and tangible the action of God within the community at any given moment and challenge it to action in the world in a spirit of loving service.

CHAPTER 9

Sin and Reconciliation

Many people have lost the sense of sin because society has social-ised them into a rugged individualism that has stripped the con-cept of love as personal long-term commitment to others of any significant meaning. Selfishness and greed have been legitimised. The notion of community has been destroyed. In such a climate, what I want, irrespective of the good of others, is what matters. If I lie, cheat, steal, commit adultery, what matter for I am simply pleasing myself and satisfying my own cravings? Having lost the sense of what it means to be a member of a community and of my obligations to that community, all that remains is my own satis-faction. Here we are at the root of the problem concerning the loss of a sense of sin and why the Sacrament of Reconciliation is in crisis. Listen to the opinions of some Sixth Year students.

'I think confession is absolutely stupid. I don't see why you should have to go and tell a priest all the little sins that you have done. Maybe it takes a weight off some peoples minds, but not mine. How can everything be all right after you have confessed? If God is reckoned to watch over you, then he knows what you have done. You can ask forgiveness there and then. Not in a confession box.'

'I believe that God will forgive you himself. I haven't been to con-fession in years as I feared going. I felt guilty and ashamed and I seemed to never tell the exact truth in case the priest would for-ever avoid me and talk about me. I confess directly to God and he has his own ways of making you do penance!'

'Confession has no meaning for me! I would go about twice a year but mainly to please my parents.'

'My view is that confession is dead for young people. By that I don't mean kids but those under thirty. Most don't believe in having to go. It's only a way of easing your guilt.'

'I don't think it's a sacrament that works.'

Sin is a religious word which, in the Bible, is any wrongdoing that God disapproves of and condemns. In the final analysis, it is something that causes human beings to suffer. It is an offence against God because it is an offence against the human person. He who is love takes what human beings do to themselves and to one another, especially the poor and weak, as done to himself. Sin is about causing excessive suffering; about making people suffer, allowing them to suffer or ignoring their suffering.

A Christian is a member of a community that is centred on and has come to know and love Christ and strives, in his Spirit, to alleviate the sufferings of humanity and reunite it in love. In such a community the primary law is the commandment of love. But love is always a gamble where I risk the deepest part of myself. There are no guarantees to cover this gamble. Others can move away from me, die, drift into a superficial relationship or into infidelity or I can move away from them. One either accepts or rejects love. For this reason every act of love is an act of trust, an act of faith. The Christian knows that that trust is well placed, that God always responds positively to our love, that it is never lost but helps build the new earth in ways that we do not always understand.

Love is what binds the community together and enables it to carry out its mission. But that love can be fractured. By the sufferings I cause or ignore, I can fracture the unity of the community or I can betray its mission by my sinfulness towards those who are not Christians.

When I sin I offend God because I cause suffering to those whom he loves. Hence in order to be reconciled to God, I have to be reconciled with those whom I have caused to suffer. In the Sacrament of Reconciliation the priest represents not just Christ but the whole body of Christ in all its members. I seek reconciliation with the members of the body whom I have offended or with the whole body if I have betrayed its mission to those outside it. This is why I confess to a priest and not just silently in my own heart. My reconciliation is with the Body of Christ. The public sign of my intention to be reconciled is my confession. The sign that the body of Christ accepts this reconciliation is the granting of absolution. The privatisation of religion has tended to denude the sacrament of this essential communitarian dimension and is one reason why it is a sacrament that 'does not seem to work'.

A further reason why this sacrament does not make sense to many young people is that very childish notions about the nature of sin have been propagated among Catholics. In the Catholic tradition, serious sin can only be committed where there is grave matter, full knowledge and full consent. The degree to which people know what they are doing and give consent to it determines their degree of guilt or responsibility for what happens. The gravity of the matter is to be measured by the amount of pain and suffering that it causes.

Sin is often reduced to the transgression of some prohibition or taboo. Contrition is seen as a desire to escape punishment (purgatory or hell). While this way of thinking may be appropriate to children who operate on an instinctual level and are reared with prohibitions accompanied by punishments and rewards, it is hardly appropriate to adults who have come to know a God who loves them at all times and under all conditions. Even when Catholics rise above this childish perception and begin to see themselves as people with powers of reason and free will, they may see sin as a matter of not being true to their own personal growth. They have let themselves and others down! Then contrition is seen as the resolve not to let themselves or others down in the future.

There is, however, another level of awareness. I can see myself called to more than my own personal development but rather called by Christ to self-transcendence, to give myself in love to others; to reach out to them and share with them; to become part

68

of a community that gives itself in service to a suffering world. Personal growth is now not just a matter of some calculated process, but a leap of faith by which I commit myself to others and draw strength from them, enriched above my own abilities and able to do things that I could not do on my own. At this level, there is an invitation to forgo my self-centredness and self pre-occupation and go out to others in love. My obligation at this level of awareness, is to work out with others what God is urging us to do as a community as we choose between various good possible options in trying to bring love and justice to the world. Guilt and Sin are then a matter of saying no to love. Contrition and con-fession are the desire for and the re-establishment of dialogue and union with others in the Christian community, the Body of Christ, and hence with God.

While sin is always personal, something I do or fail to do, it does have social consequences. There is a cartoon about the Vietnam war with captions that run as follows:
'I only deliver the goods.'
'I only help load the plane.'
'I only give clearance for take-off.'
'I only pilot the aircraft.'
'I only press the button.'
The last caption shows the Vietnamese villagers saying
'And we get killed by the bomb.'

Individual's sins can become institutionalised into the customs, laws and structures of society. Apartheid is a case in point. Governments that ignore the sufferings of their people, that trample on their human rights, that torture their citizens, are act-ing sinfully. If people are tempted to accept what such govern-ments do and knowingly go along with it they become sinners also. Members of a Trade Union or professional association may, with an easy conscience, feel quite free to pursue their 'legitimate claims' for higher wages or fringe benefits irrespective of the effect this will have on those who are poor and have no union to fight for them. A nation state or multi-national corporation may feel entitled to exploit the natural resources of the Third World countries to safeguard its profits while impoverishing millions. The suffering that results from poverty, hunger, unemployment, famine and war, is often caused by the decision of those with economic, political or cultural power who use it to serve their own 'enlightened self-interest'. The bible calls this 'the power of evil in the world'.

In the Jewish Testament one finds the prophets condemning not only the sins of individuals but also the sins of nations and empires. People experienced sin as individuals when they were unfaithful to God but they also experienced themselves as sinned against when other powerful empires attacked or enslaved them or when they were oppressed by their own leaders. Nations were thought of as having their own spirit or angel and so when any nation was cruel and oppressive, its god was seen as having become demon, a devil or an evil spirit. St Paul spoke of such corporate evil as principalities and powers, thrones, lordships or the rulers of this world. When Israel was threatened by outside powers, they were referred to as the gods of this world, as Satan. Satan became the symbol of a universal experience of evil. The principalities and powers spoken of by Paul represented the evil embedded in the structures of society which were threatening and cruel.

One of the great insights of the Jewish Testament was that a suffering people could give prophetic witness to the world. The people – represented as the Suffering Servant – gave prophetic witness through their suffering because it cried out for justice. In Christian times, Jesus came to be seen as the Suffering Servant representing all those who were oppressed, outcasts of their society, dehumanised in any way. When one contemplates Jesus on the cross, one sees what society did to him and to the people he represented. When one sees Jesus on the cross today one sees all those who suffer from 'man's inhumanity to man' in our society and in our world.

But very often sin is blind. The blindness of the Pharisees, for example, is a common theme in the New Testament. They were concerned with upholding a system of purity and holiness which Jesus denounced because he felt compassion for those who suffered under it. 'Some Pharisees and teachers of the Law came from Jerusalem to Jesus and asked him, 'Why is it that your disciples disobey the teaching handed down by our ancestors? They don't wash their hands in the proper way before they eat!' Jesus answered, 'And why do you disobey God's command and follow your own teaching? For God said, 'respect your father and mother', and 'whoever curses his father or his mother is to be put to death.' But you teach that if a person has something he could use to help his father or mother, but says, 'This belongs to God', he does not need to honour his father or mother. In this way you disregard God's command, in order to follow your own teaching. You hypocrites!' (Mt 15:1-7) Such blindness is a form of culpable ignorance. The Pharisees did not want to see the suffering caused by their teachings. An individual or a group can be blind to the effects of its actions and the suffering they cause, like the alcoholic whose pleasure in drink blinds him to the misery and suffering he is causing to those around him, not to mention the damage he is doing to himself. However, those who suffer from his alcoholism are not blind as they experience the effects of his problem through their suffering. They know what sin is for they suffer its consequences. Similarly the poor, the unemployed, those forced to emigrate, those maimed by paramilitaries in Northern Ireland suffer the consequences of Governments' or group blindness.

I have a young friend who suffers a rare disease called arthryogryphosis. He was born with a twisted body; torso, arms and legs. He has very limited use of his hands and over the years he has had major surgery to put rods in his back to protect his spine. He has had his legs amputated and is totally dependent for all his needs on his foster mother. From the neck up he is bright, intelligent, witty and courageous. The State, however, provides totally inadequate funding to help him lead as normal a life as possible for someone in his condition. He is typical of many

71

handicapped people in our society. In a word, he is the victim of corporate sinfulness: the decisions taken by those in power to prioritise other ways of spending taxpayers money, causing suffering to those in greatest need. Whenever the state allows people to suffer or fails to alleviate their suffering, then it is acting sinfully and they become the victims of corporate sin. It is not just a matter of transgressing some law but a transgression of the divine call to love.

The Christian answer to sin and the suffering that results from it is the Cross, that most shocking form of execution known to the ancient world. The cross was the great symbol of power used by the Romans to deter anyone who might contemplate opposition to their rule. Pilate may have consented to Jesus' execution because he thought that he wanted to make himself King of the Jews and overthrow the system of government which the Romans used to rule their vassal state. But the reason Jesus died on the cross was because he was shocked by the suffering he encountered among the poor and because he was determined to do something about it. He shared the lot of the oppressed, by choice, and when he opposed the oppressors he paid the price. Jesus taught the brother/sisterhood of all. Rich and poor, countryman and foreigner were all children of the one Father and power was to be used to serve the needs of all, not the selfish interests of the few: a message the oppressors did not want to hear and why they had Jesus done to death.

In one sense Jesus' mission was a failure. He did not achieve his life's ambition of winning all to his idea of the need for a change of heart so that God's love would reign in the hearts of all men and women. But in another vital sense Jesus death was a success because it led to the creation of a new people, the Church. Evil men tried to destroy Jesus but he rose again in a new body which is the people of God. St Paul spells this out time and again. 'All of you are Christ's body, and each one is a part of it.' (1 Cor 12:27). The Church is Christ's body, the completion of him who himself completes all things everywhere.' (Eph 1:28) 'We are members of

Christ's body.' *(Eph 5:30)* 'And now I (Paul) am happy about my sufferings for you, for by means of my physical suffering I am helping to complete what still remains of Christ's sufferings on behalf of his body, the Church.' *(Col 1:24)*.

The Community called Church is the body of Christ, there to carry on the mission of Christ, even to suffer as he suffered as it offers its life in sacrifice for the salvation of the world. Defending the poor and those who suffer, pleading their cause, siding with them for their rights, giving them back a sense of their dignity as children of God, is to continue the work of the risen Christ and 'complete what still remains of Christ's sufferings'.

The poor, the handicapped, the marginalised, the oppressed from the point of departure for Christian communities wishing to be recreated in the image of Christ. Here is where I as an individual and where each Christian community needs conversion and reconciliation. To experience such conversion we must be with the poor for some time at least, listening to them and sharing some of their experience and suffering. If we start from the poor, as Jesus did, we can help build a more just society: help build the Kingdom. Wherever we are in the class system, rich, middle class or poor we have a particular way of feeling, thinking, being with and celebrating with our friends. To be 'poor in spirit' is not to be condescending but means making real friends with the poor *(Rom 12:16)* who need us just as the Jewish people needed Moses who, through his experience of the Egyptian government system, understood how the Empire worked and knew how to go about freeing his people from slavery.

As a Christian community we need healing from our blindness with regard to those who suffer in our midst and we need to learn the nature of total self-giving in the spirit of Jesus. Total self-giving means not being entrenched; not simply guarding and protecting what we have; not extending all our energies on keeping the institution alive or expanding it. To be 'poor in spirit' means casting off some of our links with those who have power and opening our eyes to the world and people around us: opening our hearts and ourselves to their most immediate needs and responding to their needs in the integral way Jesus did. To respond to human needs out of love is to evangelise; is to bring Good News into the lives of others.

When a community undergoes conversion and begins to know and befriend the poor or those who are marginalised in any way by listening to them, getting to know how they feel, think, suffer and celebrate and begins to act with them on their behalf, then it becomes a truly Christian community. It has undergone repentance and conversion and is reconciled with Christ's poor.

There is no doubt that this is a difficult task, giving rise to all sorts of fears especially for middle-class people who tend to be concerned with their self-preservation and are often unwilling to face the challenge of deprivation and unemployment in their midst. It is only when they make the effort to get into genuine contact with those who suffer that they begin to feel in their 'guts' that something has to be done. Conversion takes place much more in the heart than in the head. If I mix only with those of my own class or those who are well off I will never feel this compassion that Jesus felt but will see the poor and marginalised as people on the other side of a very large fence.

When a Christian community takes such conversion seriously it can expect opposition. The words of Jesus take on greater significance. 'If the world hates you, just remember that it has hated me first. If you belonged to the world, then the world would love you as its own ... If they persecuted me, they will persecute you too.' (Jn 15:18, 20).

When sin is seen in this wider communitarian context, it ceases to be reduced to 'I didn't say my morning or evening prayers' or 'I had bad thoughts but I didn't take pleasure in them'! Rather it is seen as all that causes human suffering and Reconciliation is the effort to undo that suffering by standing with the poor and marginalised in genuine solidarity.

Here is the challenge for all followers of Christ. Can they, will they stand where Christ stood in solidarity with the poor? Can they, will they form themselves into communities that follow Christ in the service of all who suffer? When the unity of the community is fractured, as it inevitably will be for no love progresses without death and resurrection, sin and repentance, will they be prepared to admit failure and begin again?

If such communities were to exist might not the Sacrament of Reconciliation take on a new and vital meaning for some young people at least and counteract that rugged individualism which now denudes the notion of sin of any meaning for so many of them?

If people, and particularly the young, were to find themselves members of a genuine community that struggled together to find God's will in their daily lives; that created a climate of stillness and prayer for itself in the midst of the world's turmoil; that searched the scriptures together for light and direction as to how to proceed in terms of relationships and action on behalf of the 'broken' so beloved of Christ; then they might find themselves belonging to a genuine Christian community that could celebrate sacramentally in a way that made sense and would no longer be 'boring'.

The Church has to continually rediscover for itself the import of Christ and his message and what it means to be a Christian Community sharing in the life-giving mission of Jesus today. This is no easy task but, as Jesus put it, 'If anyone wants to be a follower of mine let him take up his cross daily and follow me.'

Can schools help?

PART III

Good News and
The Murder Machine

The conditions we should strive to bring about in our education system are not the conditions favourable to the rapid and cheap manufacturing of ready-mades but the conditions favourable to the growth of living organisms.

(Patrick Pearse: *The Murder Machine*)

CHAPTER 10

Believing in the Young

Irish schools are at a crossroads. In the past they educated pupils from Christian families who, by and large, remained loyal to their Christian traditions all their lives. Today these same schools seem to be failing in their mission and many parents and teachers are at a loss to know why.

The problem, of course, is simply a reflection of what is happening in society. The privatisation of religion, the breakdown in community, rampant consumerism and rugged individualism all challenge the very *raison d'etre* of Christian schools. So how can such schools come to terms with what has happened? How can they bring the Good News of Christ to young people today?

Effective Christian schools will be genuine communities where the spirit of Christ permeates all that happens within the school. The spirit of Christ will affect not only the way teachers teach and pupils learn but also the way teachers interact with one another and with management.

Christianity has to be 'caught' not just 'taught' and God is to be found in all that goes on in the school, not just in formal religion classes or liturgies but within the entire reality of pupils' and teachers' daily lives.

To be effective, parents and teachers have to believe in young people; not always an easy task as parents and teachers know only too well. Young people know how to irritate adults. If adults value neatness, they will be untidy and mess up their rooms and wear the latest 'objectionable' haircut. If adults insist on good

78

manners, they will interrupt and use bad language. If adults like good books, they will read comics. If adults believe in going to Church, they will claim they are atheists. Parents and teachers are at a loss to know what to do and somehow act predictably. First they try to be in command and act tough. When this fails they try kindness. When this fails they try reasoning. When reason fails, they try ridicule and rebuke. When this fails they get back to threats and punishment and all end up as members of a mutual frustration society!

An oriental proverb advises relaxation in face of the inevitable! Adolescence is a time of stress, strain and turmoil. Rebellion against authority and against convention is to be expected and tolerated for the sake of growth and learning. It is not easy, however, to watch young sir turn into an unruly adolescent. Parents often do not know what is happening when he lies on his bed, staring into space and find it bewildering to watch his shifting moods or listen to his never ending complaints. Nothing satisfies him. The house is grotty, the car is a heap of junk, Mum and Dad are old fashioned, the school stinks, the food is terrible. He is behind in his work and his language is crude. He quarrels with his brothers and sisters and ignores what parents say. Have faith in young people!

But there is method in his madness. He is growing up. His personality is undergoing the required changes: from organisation (childhood) through disorganisation (adolescence) to reorganisation (adulthood). Every young person has to reform her personality and free herself from childhood ties with parents and teachers, establish new links with her contemporaries and find her own identity. He can be concerned with unanswerable questions; be obsessed with the fragility of life and the inevitability of death. She can be tormented with terrors that seem private and personal, not realising the universality of such doubts.

'Adolescence cannot be a perpetually happy time. It is a time for uncertainty, self-doubt and suffering. This is the age of cosmic yearnings and private passions, of social concern and personal agony. It is the age of inconsistency and ambivalence. As Anna Freud put it: 'It is normal for an adolescent to behave in an inconsistent manner; to fight his impulses and to accept them; to love his parents and to hate them; to be deeply ashamed to acknowledge his mother before others and, unexpectedly, to desire heart-to-heart talks with her; to thrive on imitation of and identification with others while searching unceasingly for his own identity; to be more idealistic, artistic, generous, and unselfish than he will ever be again but also the opposite: self-centred, egotistic, calculating. Such fluctuations between extreme opposites would be thought abnormal at any other time of life. At this time they may signify no more than that an adult structure of personality takes a long time to emerge; that the ego of the individual in question does not cease to experiment and is in no hurry to close down possibilities.' It is no use asking a teenager, 'What's the matter with you? Why can't you sit still? What's come over you?' These are unanswerable questions. Even if he knew, he could not say: 'Look Mum, I'm torn by conflicting emotions. I'm engulfed by irrational urges. I'm burning with unfamiliar desires.' (Quoted in *Between Parent and Teenager*, Dr Haim G. Hinnot, Cassell, London 1973.)

Parents and teachers can help by accepting young people as they are; by tolerating their restlessness, respecting their loneliness, accepting their discontent and by not prying. Acceptance is paramount. To accept young people as they are is important in fostering a relationship in which they can grow, develop, make constructive changes, learn to solve problems, move in the direction of emotional health and become more productive and creative. It is one of the simple paradoxes of life that when people feel they are truly accepted, then they are free to begin to think about how they want to change, to grow and become different.

Acceptance is like the good soil that permits the wheat to grow and develop to the full. The soil enables the seed to become wheat. It releases the capacity to grow, but the capacity is entirely within the seed, implanted there by God. As with the seed, so young people contain entirely within themselves the capacity to develop. If adults provide the soil of acceptance, young people are enabled to grow and mature. As parents or teachers we often fail to understand the positive effects of acceptance. Most people are brought up to believe that if we accept a young person as she is she will just remain that way; that the best way to help her become something better in the future is to tell her what we do not accept about her now.

So in rearing and educating young people, many adults rely heavily on language of unacceptance, believing that this is the best way to help them. The soil that adults often provide for young people is heavy with evaluation, judgment, criticism, preaching, admonishing and commanding; messages that convey the impression that they do not accept young people as they are. But evaluating, judging and criticising turn young people off. They stop talking to adults and soon learn that it is more comfortable to keep their feelings and problems to themselves.

Of all the effects of acceptance none is as important to young people as the feeling that they are loved in spite of all the inner and outer turmoil that is going on in their lives. To accept someone as she is is truly an act of love; to feel accepted is to feel loved and being loved promotes growth of body and mind and is probably the most effective force we know for repairing both psychological and even physical damage.

Acceptance is not simply a passive attitude but has to be demonstrated. Mother Teresa of Calcutta once advised 'Listen to your children more'. It is the key to many parents and teachers problems with young people. Giving time to listen to young people is the primary way of demonstrating our acceptance. For most adults the giving of such time requires a lot of patience, tolerance and selflessness.

To be an effective listener there are several 'musts' one has to observe. One must really want to share what a young person has to say. One must genuinely want to be with her when she desires to talk. One must be able to accept her feelings, whatever they may be or however different they may be from one's own or from the feelings one thinks she 'should' feel. One must have a deep trust in the young person's capacity to handle her own feelings, to work through them, to find solutions to her problems and this trust is acquired by actually watching her do that. One must appreciate that feelings are transitory, that they change. Hate can turn to love, discouragement may be quickly replaced by hope. One need not be afraid of feelings getting expressed; they will not become forever fixed inside the young person. Finally, one must be able to see the young person as separate, a unique person. This is particularly true for parents. A child is a separate individual to whom they have given life. Acknowledging this 'separateness' enables parents to 'permit' young people have their own feelings and their own way of perceiving things. What is true for parents is also true for teachers.

By listening to young people and how they think and feel, teachers and parents run the risk of having their opinions and attitudes changed. To be open to another person, especially one we think we know but often do not, invites the possibility of having to interpret our own experience. This can be challenging. A defensive person cannot afford to expose himself to ideas and views that are different from his own. A flexible person is not afraid of being changed. All young people who have flexible parents and teachers respond positively when they see their mothers, fathers and teachers willing to change, to learn, to be human.

While young people are, by and large, non-conformists who call everything into question, yet they inject dynamism into the world. They tend to be very sensitive to social problems. They demand authenticity and simplicity, and they rebelliously reject a society invaded by all sorts of hypocrisy. This dynamism makes them capable of renewing cultures that otherwise would grow decrepit, and of bringing hope to the world. The creative dynamism of young people is blocked when adults are neither authentic nor open to dialogue with them. When they are not taken seriously, they move out in different directions. Some take to various radical ideologies because of their natural idealism. Some just become indifferent to all that is going on around them. What disorients young people most is the threat to their need for authenticity by adults who tend to be inconsistent and even manipulative; by the generation-gap conflict; by a consumer civilisation and by a drugs, sex and alcohol culture.

The family is the primary community in which young people are born and raised. Its stability, way of relating to young people, lifestyle, and openness to young people's values play a large role in the success or failure of young people to achieve fulfilment in life. The same is essentially true of schools where young people expand their knowledge of the world and come to terms with their role in it.

CHAPTER 11

The Teacher as Educator

People tend to forget much of what they learned in the classroom but do remember the sort of teachers they had when they were at school. Good teachers, the ones we tend to remember, are educators in the broadest sense of the term and not simply people who see the task of education as merely passing on information or preparing young people for examinations or the world of work.

The role of a Christian educator is to help open the eyes of students to the wonders of God's world. There are those, of course, who see the world as 'secular', as having little or nothing to do with God. For such people, especially those whose religion is 'world-denying', the sacred or the spiritual is above or beyond ordinary day to day living. They do not seem to have settled into Vatican II's vision of the world as a place where 'God's Spirit, who with a marvellous providence directs the unfolding of time and renews the face of the earth, is not absent from its development'. While one cannot take an over-optimistic view of the world which is also full of totalitarian nightmares, of nuclear arsenals, labour camps, torture chambers and famine, nonetheless it is within the world and its history that God is to be found. God is the author of all reality, all truth and all knowledge and is present and working in all creation: in nature, in history and in each human being. So Christian education affirms the radical goodness of the world 'charged with the grandeur of God', to use Hopkins' phrase, and it regards every element of creation as worthy of study and contemplation, capable of endless exploration that can lead to an appreciation of the Creator.

There are two ways in which a teacher, can relate positively to the world. The first sees knowledge as serving mastery and control. This is the attitude of the user (and so open to abuse). The second is a subjective one, an attitude of reverence, of worship (and so open to idolatry). In the first objective way of relating to the world, one sees it as the object of study. Nature, and the laws by which it operates; peoples and their ways of life; the social, economic, political, cultural structures of society; history; the web of relationships; the achievements and failures of humanity; the good and evil in human evolution – these are what teachers try to help students to understand with a thorough and sound intellectual formation which includes a growing ability to reason reflectively, logically and critically. All this happens through careful and sustained study based on competent and well-motivated teaching. Teachers seek to ensure that the mind of the student is informed and not so deformed by being limited to any one way of knowing that it cannot or will not remain open to all winds of truth from whatever direction they blow. The Spirit of God is active in every human and physical activity, always creating and healing, a spirit of life and wisdom, and Christian education tries to make that awareness explicit.

The second way of relating to the world is the subjective attitude of reverence for the least of all things, an attitude of wonder and mystery. The objects of the world do more than witness to their Creator, to God's wisdom and power, they induce wonder. Karl Rahner said: 'We live on the beach of an infinite sea of mystery occupied with the grains of sand we find there.' To convey a sense of wonder to a student, teachers have to lift their eyes from the 'grains of sand'. But they may be faced with one great problem. Students minds have often been ossified in positivism, for today's progress in science and technology can foster a certain emphasis on observable data and an agnosticism about everything else. However, there is a way forward. Literature and the Arts are of great importance for they try to probe the unique nature of men and women, their problems, and their experiences as they struggle to know and perfect themselves and the world.

Literature and the arts are preoccupied with revealing peoples' place in history, with illustrating their miseries and joys, their needs and strengths, and with foreshadowing a better life. It is often poets and artists rather than theologians, philosophers or scientists who allow us to taste life in the spirit. Blake can 'see a world in a grain of sand'. For Elizabeth Browning 'Every bush is afire with God'. The educator is full of worship for the mystery hidden and revealed in what God has created and is not just an information giver but one who has learnt to wonder and evoke wonder in the young.

As young people learn to think about themselves and their world, the educational process should enable them to speak for themselves. In today's world so dominated by the communications media, the development of effective communication skills is more necessary than ever before. This is particularly true for the poor. 'A characteristic of our urban poor is a sense of powerlessness. It is more acutely felt in the poorest areas of the city, where people cannot reach the subtle levers of power that middle class citizens take for granted – money, a good address, influence, status, access to lawyers and accountants, the ability to write 'office' letters and use the telephone. In such a situation you have the vote but have probably long time despaired of politics. You probably subsist on a low income or are dependent on social security payments. You live in below standard rented property, and send your children to overcrowded nineteenth century schools. Little by little, you retreat into silence and depression, the 'apathy' of the urban poor.

It is common to hear professionals – teachers, planners, clergy, social workers – bemoan the apathy of young people. 'They are not interested'; 'they will not help themselves'; 'no one is bothered' – are common comments. Beneath this cloak of indifference, beneath the protective shell of apathy, there is a deep feeling of futility, of an inability to change anything. In other words, people in our deprived areas feel powerless because they see themselves as the object of other people's decisions.' (Brian Wren: *Education for Justice*) One function of Christian education is to enable such people to make their voices heard.

Each student is a person and each personality is incommunicable. The student is not just a statistical unit, 'part of a class', but an irreplaceable human being. Just as people can reverence nature for its reflection of the Creator, so one reverences the student for his or her incommunicable and unique mirroring of God. One's relationship to the pupil is a one-to-one, an I-Thou relationship. In the classroom it may have to become an I-You relationship as circumstances can make the person-to-person encounter impossible. But it is never an I-Them confrontation. If education were only the 'passing on of information', a mere lecturing process, then this might not be the case. Somehow or other teachers need to be able to exercise this vital factor of their vocation, – the awareness and acceptance of the student as a private mystery of infinite worth. Another way of putting this is is to say that teachers possess a faith that sees doing justice as an integral part of their vocation. To do justice, from the perspective of Jesus, is to treat others as unique human beings.

Above all else students are entitled to love. 'To love is not to give of your riches but to reveal to others their riches, their gifts, their value and to trust them and their capacity to grow'. *(Jean Vanier)* To treat students as people of infinite worth because of their dignity as sons and daughters of God is to do them justice. There is also the hope that if teachers do this students may learn this vital lesson also.

If teachers are not willing to give this kind of reverential love to their students, quite simply their response to the Creative Spirit of God is defective precisely where it should be evident and active. If they cannot see students with the eyes of faith and cannot go beyond the justice of a 'fair day's work for a fair day's pay' to the justice that gives reverence in love, they are simply in the wrong school!

By love, appreciation and affirmation, students are helped to grow. All students no matter how weak academically, how broken through home circumstances, need to be challenged but also allowed to be themselves, loved, helped to grow and discover their particular gifts and the fact that life has more meaning than watching TV or even learning mathematics!

Nor is this student-centred approach to education simply an abdication of responsibility for school discipline. Any teacher has a responsibility to set standards and demonstrate values. Teenagers need to know what they respect and what they expect. Of course, they will oppose standards, resist the rules and test teachers' limits. This is as it should be. No one can mature by blindly obeying parents or teachers. Teachers expect teenagers to resent the rules! They are not expected to like prohibitions. However, there is a crucial difference between imposing restrictions and setting limits. In the past teenagers' feelings were often ignored. Restrictions were laid down in anger and argument and in a language that invited resistance. In a more constructive approach, limits are set in a manner that preserves teenagers self-respect. The limits are neither arbitrary nor capricious. They are anchored in values and aimed at character building.

The distinction between feelings and actions is the cornerstone of the proper approach to teenagers and discipline. Teachers are permissive when dealing with feelings and wishes. They are strict when dealing with unacceptable behaviour. They respect teenager's opinions and attitudes and do not belittle their dreams and desires, but reserve the right to stop and redirect some of their acts because they are concerned enough and strong enough to endure their temporary animosity when they must uphold standards and values that protect them and society.

Overall, the response of a teacher to the creative spirit of God involves a sense of serious professional responsibility; an openness to others and their particular responses to the same Spirit; a positive acceptance of the world and its concerns; a worship of creation as coming from God; reverence for the person of the student and an openness to truth, to the unfathomable mystery of life and being or however one wants to conceive the spiritual dimension of life. In this way they can be bearers of Good News, helping students take one small step in the process of becoming more human, a process of infinite value.

Their mission is to bring Good News to young people. They do this by helping young people overcome the slavery of ignorance and by encouraging and fostering in them the pursuit of truth which can lead towards the fullness of humanity. Genuine education is not about digesting bucketfuls of information to be regurgitated in examinations but about human growth.

Just as God is at work in a tree, giving it life, sustaining it, helping it to grow, so God is at work in each human being, giving life, sustaining it and enabling each person to develop and grow into the fullness of his or her unique humanity. God is in each individual not just in the sense that she is created by God and then left to her own devices but in the sense that God, a powerful personal force outside humanity, acts as a great inner personalising force nurturing each human being towards the fullness of her humanity so that, in the end, she can become like God and be at one with the Love Event that is God. A teacher's vocation is to facilitate this personalising force in the lives of young people.

CHAPTER 12

Towards a Philosophy
of Christian Education

One of the problems with our educational system is that there is no overt philosophy underpining it, and those responsible for educational planning in recent years have simply sidestepped the issue. This is not to say that various philosophies of education are inoperative. Competitiveness, individualism, consumerism and pragmatism are the hallmarks of recent Irish educational planning. Schools that want to promote a Christian philosophy need to be aware of these operative values and consciously plan to counteract them.

Schools today have to come to grips not only with an unprecedented rate of growth in knowledge and technology but with fundamental changes in current beliefs, values and standards of behaviour. This is bound to make the definition of an acceptable philosophy enormously more difficult than it was in the past. But unless the school community, in the widest sense, knows what the school's deepest aspirations are, what it is trying to achieve, and how that achievement is being planned and organised, there is an obvious danger that individuals and groups will pull in opposite directions, producing confusion, cross-purposes and lack of drive and momentum.

There is also another reason why it is essential that Christian schools be clear as to what they are about: unless they clarify their philosophy for themselves, others will do the job for them. That is already happening. Today the 'points system' and third-level entry requirements, the demands of employers and of government are what determine the actual philosophy of many schools. The primary concern of these groups is not the development of the full human person but rather the production of citizens who will be valuable in terms of specific skills or of future economic value to the state.

A Christian school tries to construct a working philosophy for itself when it confronts its own life and work with the life-giving Good News of Jesus – that all men and women, especially the poorest and the weakest, are brothers and sisters in Christ, children of a loving father and are to be treated as such – and seeks to make this Good News operative in its own day to day operation.

A Christian school is not just a 'points factory' but sees its mission as directed away from itself towards the service of the wider society outside its own doors. Just as the Church does not exist for itself and is not there to be served, but to serve, so a Christian school community is there to serve society by instilling in its students the ideal that they are being educated to be 'men and women for others', able and willing to make a positive contribution towards building up the world in justice and love.

A school community is a restricted number of educators, students, parents and administrators who ideally share a common philosophy of education. 'If we are going to use the word (community) meaningfully we must restrict it to a group of individuals who have learned how to communicate honestly with each other, whose relationships go deeper than their masks of composure, and who have developed some significant commitment to rejoice together, mourn together and to delight in each other, make others' condition our own.' *(M. Scott Peck)*

One of the problems for many schools in elaborating its philosophy is the privatisation of religion. When religion is seen as only dealing with 'spiritual' matters, (personal guilt and salvation from guilt), educators fail to see its connection to other dimensions of school life. (What, for example, does the gospel have to say to science or business studies, football or French?) If staff members are to share a Christian philosophy and a sense of mission together, they have to be prepared to share where they are at in relation to the Christian faith and elaborate a corporate vision for the school. This will demand honest communication about one's faith and its relationship to everyday life. This does not happen easily (especially if one has doubts about aspects of the faith or fears for one's job if one admits to such doubts) but without it a Christian school community will be such only in name. Trying to elaborate a vision for the school may entail a real 'dying to self', since it calls for an acceptance of values that run counter to the prevailing culture. As they seek to elaborate the school's philosophy, educators may have to undergo a constant change of heart and mind ('repentance') as they listen to their colleagues and share their understanding of the gospel. Such sharing is never easy but it does evoke an atmosphere of realism, humility and healing. A staff that honestly engages in trying to elaborate its philosophy, through sincere and open communication, is not subject to mob psychology. Individuals are free to speak their minds and be listened to. A staff of thirty or forty usually comes up with differing viewpoints and, as a result, the consensus that emerges is usually more creative than something imposed from the top. Because a community of mind and heart is being formed, and people feel free to express their differing points of view, they come to appreciate the aims and objectives of the school far better than an individual on her own can do. In striving to shape its corporate vision, a staff will work out of many frames of reference and experience disagreements, misunderstanding and misinterpretations, but in seeking to overcome these, its conclusions will be all the more rounded because they approach reality more closely.

Individualism is one of the great sins of modern society and educators do not escape from it either! Individualism predisposes one to arrogance, but when people begin to try to elaborate a corporate vision, they begin to appreciate the gifts and talents as well as the limitations of others, as well as their own. When I see other people's difficulties and share their problems, I can accept my own limitations as well. This can lead to a genuine sense of humility but also to a sense of hope, because the pooled talents of all can compensate for the limitations of others and make for a creative ambience in which to work.

In elaborating a Christian philosophy, creative community building begins. People start to feel free to be themselves and not to have to assume attitudes and poses. In such an atmosphere, old wounds can be healed and old resentments forgiven. The sins of the past, by religious or lay, can be admitted and the school can move on from there. When people start to accept one another as they are, accepting both their limitations and their talents, healing and conversion take place automatically. When I stop trying to convert others to my ways of thinking, or trying to heal or change them, but accept them as they are, then they are free to be themselves, free to discard those masks they use to hide their own inadequacies or keep others at bay, free to seek their psychological and spiritual health in an atmosphere of trust.

To achieve such communication (and it has been achieved in some schools) means giving time, effort and commitment to one another, which teachers are often afraid to do out of fear or apathy. Commitment of people to one another in searching for a common vision is a crucial factor in building community. If communication is open, individuals will be able to speak their minds and even go against the trend, but the resulting vision, born of many differing viewpoints, will be more effective than one or two people alone prescribing what that philosophy should be because a wider view of the gospel is gained than can be achieved by the few. Such a task will involve struggle: the struggle to overcome individualism and apathy; the struggle to discern the will of God in the here and now; the struggle, above all, to involve the poorest and weakest members of the school community in its mission.

Such a community is like a living organism, like a vine and its branches. Such an image suggests a human organisation where people, united to Christ, work together in harmony and solidarity to achieve what no individual can achieve alone. Working together is what gives Christians their strength and solidarity but this involves 'taking up the cross', and overcoming a 'mé féin' mentality which is always a difficult challenge as people tend to rely solely on their own view of the world, 'do their own thing', and not want to have to take account of group decisions. Jesus challenges his followers to overcome such individualism and work together. 'Where two or three are gathered together in my name, I am there in their midst.' Christians are to be known by the love they have for one another, but being an effective community member will always entail 'laying down one's life for the sake of others'.

Another factor that has to be faced in Irish schools is that many lay Christians, over the past fifty or sixty years, have felt themselves to be second-class citizens, especially in Catholic schools, hired to 'fill-in' when no religious was available for a post. Gradually, since the second Vatican Council and with the fall in religious vocations, lay educators have come to play a greater role in Catholic schools. But the idea persists that lay people have been reluctantly given such roles only because there are no longer any religious to fill them. It would be idle to deny that this is even the way some religious themselves have seen the situation. Religious have to admit their sins of the past.

Beneath these facts, however, there lies a deeper reality. The Church is providentially being forced to re-examine the role of lay men and women and this is reflected in what is happening in schools. That religious vocations have fallen in the western world is a fact of history, but God speaks through history and may be ushering in a new age when men and women will take their rightful places as the bearers of the Good News to present and future generations. Furthermore, there is a growing recognition that co-operation between religious and laity is not a last ditch effort to preserve and maintain Christian schools, but a challenge to gather different gifts and put them to the best possible use in order to bring the Good News of Christ, in all its fullness, to young people. The historical role that lay people have had to play in religious run schools sometimes makes it difficult now to engage them in shaping a Christian philosophy of education. Only honest and open communication and admission of the wrongs of the past can help solve this problem.

A philosophy alone, however, is not enough to build a genuinely Christian school community. There also has to be a sharing of power and responsibility. Unless those in charge of the school are prepared to share responsibility, educators will remain in a subordinate position, see themselves as mere 'employees' and have no reason to help elaborate the school's vision or inculcate it among students. But if there is a sharing of responsibility without a shared philosophy, there is a danger of politicisation and a struggle for power as people try to impose their particular vision on how the school should operate. How often one comes across such divisions in staff rooms! The Principal is seen as 'the boss' (and may see herself!) while staff jockey for power by withholding cooperation in some vital areas of school life.

If a school is to be truly Christian, another model of operation has to be found. For the Christian, authority is seen in terms of service, not raw power. Administrators are there to serve the unity of the school community, not to dominate it. To achieve unity of purpose, those with authority involve staff members in elaborating the vision of the school and in the decision-making process, otherwise a 'them and us' syndrome will prevail, leading to disunity, conflict and betrayal of the gospel.

To create a school community is a challenge requiring courage and the overcoming of many fears. If people are serious about it, however, they will be working with the creative Spirit of God as they try to build an ethos where young people can be helped to grow and mature. This is a noble vocation, no matter how underrated teachers often feel themselves to be!

But one can have no illusions about the difficulty of the task in hand. The corporate entities involved in any way in the educational process – the Department of Education, Universities, Employers Organisations, even Teacher Unions – can encourage competitiveness, individualism and selfish pragmatism; philosophies which promote a partial vision of the human person and the educational process.

Governments tend to see education as primarily serving economic goals. This was articulated by a Government commission which produced a report in 1965 called 'Investment in Education'. 'A country must seek in developing its educational system to satisfy, among other things, the manpower needs of the future. If the range and level of skills required to convert economic potential into economic achievement are not available, the country is unlikely to have the resources needed to provide education of the quality and variety that is being increasingly demanded. As education is at once a cause and a consequence of economic growth, economic planning is incomplete without educational planning. Education, as well as having its own intrinsic values, is a necessary element in economic development.' Since that report, educational policies have been closely linked with economic planning. The Department of Education, for example, urges the teaching of technology, computer studies or German, so that Irish students can compete in European markets. Universities and the world of business 'use' the educational system to competitively select the people it wants for the country's future economic needs. The broader, humanising side of the educational process has largely been lost sight of and the educational process is debased as a result.

An educational system does not come into existence by itself: it is not a result of blind fate but the result of policy decisions taken by men and women who organise society in a particular way. Most people simply experience 'the system' as given. They take for granted the social climate into which they are born and, without necessarily understanding what is going on, are socialised into its values which today tend to be individualistic, selfish and competitive, with money as the final measure of everything. Things, products and possessions, are given value while people are treated as mere things or objects to be employed or made redundant as the economic climate demands. Such a society can, with a relatively easy conscience, export people as easily as goods. It can do without people but not without money, the new false god.

Society, in and through the media and the educational system, says to young people 'the important thing is to get on; be competitive, succeed. Prepare yourself to enjoy the good life; work for monetary gain; think simply in terms of a future career and see education as a means to that end. What is important is the contribution you can make to society as valued by the economic worth of your own work. People are needed to run our industries, work on the farms, serve in the hotels, keep the economy on the move, improve the gross national product'. This vision is very similar to that described by Pearse in the *Murder Machine*.

As a philosophy of education, however, it is vitally flawed not because economic development is evil but because it is stressed to the detriment of other human values. Fr Fergal O'Connor OP expressed the matter as follows: 'The society we are living in is a severely individualistic society, a society where we define people as autonomous, free individuals with rights and claims of a total kind on society. That picture of the individual finds expression in the educational system in terms of competition, aggression, achievement, domination. So you can say that what we are teaching in our so called Christian schools is little more than the very antithesis of the gospel. The real issue at stake in education is whether or not our educational system is in the interests of the person who is being educated or in the interests of some system (e.g. economic system) that is defined by somebody else or other criteria that have nothing in the world to do with personal development.'

CHAPTER 13

Models of Education

People tend to think of education as being primarily about learning a curriculum prescribed by the Department of Education. The primary function of the teacher then is simply to teach that curriculum. While a teacher may be content with such a definition, an educator certainly is not. For the educator the unfolding of the human personality in all its richness is paramount.

There are two main models of education. The first, the more traditional model, is the Transmission Model which sees education as the passing on of information, skills, values and traditions which are needed if pupils are to function adequately in society. In such a perspective, the role of the pupil is mainly passive. Education is a ceremony of initiation where a teacher introduces pupils to the knowledge that society wants them to master. It is a one-way relationship where the teacher is placed over pupils rather than accompanying them on a voyage of discovery. Secondary education is seen as preparing students for the world of work and inculcating in them the necessary social graces so that they are prepared for life in society. People who hold this view imply that a person's happiness is to be discovered through a full integration into society as it is. Hence the school mirrors the values and interests of that society and provides courses that will produce the skills demanded by it. This has been the model largely in operation in Ireland up to the present time.

While such a model may have been sustainable in fairly fixed and static societies over many generations, it is no longer useful in our constantly changing, dynamic world. Part of young people's frustration lies in the fact that they are being subjected to an outdated approach to education, one that is primarily that of information giving and where their role is one of passively memorising facts without seeing where they fit into life. Today students acquire much more information through the media than they ever do in a classroom. Radio and television have much more effect on pupils' knowledge of the world than any teacher in a secondary school and part of teachers' malaise is that, if their role is simply that of information giver, they are in a no-win situation. Furthermore, in an uncertain and constantly changing world, the mere absorption or memorisation of information is no longer enough to enable young people cope with life.

Another model of education brings us to the heart of what education is really about: personal growth or 'learning' if that word can be stretched to cover all manner of growth across the full range of the latent powers of the human personality. Real education is not just about training people for jobs or unemployment but about human growth. People who are growing in human terms will be those who will live life most successfully. After all, it is the individual human being who works, keeps firms accounts, is a TD, a member of the local branch of the GAA or someone on the dole. It is the individual human being who relates to other people; who experiences love, hate, depression, fear, sorrow, joy and hope. Human relationships go to make up the joy and sorrow content of the life of each person and, in the end, determine whether a person's life is fulfilled or not. No education worth the name will be genuine unless it takes these factors into consideration. Even from the point of view of employers or the State, the person with a rounded education would be better material for employment or be in a better position to cope with unemployment.

Genuine education, then, is about human growth and the most distinctive feature of such growth is that it comes about through wonder, thought and the ability to communicate. Thought is what shapes my inner world, my relationships with other people, with nature and ultimately with God. Because I can consciously reflect upon myself and the world, I can see things as they are and imagine what they could be. I can plan to change what I see and even put my plans into effect. But to do so I have to be able to stand back from myself and my world and inspect what I have absorbed, question what I have accepted, examine what I have been taught. I have to learn to wonder, learn to think for myself and learn to communicate. Learning to wonder, to think and to communicate effectively with others is what education is all about and it should be a liberating experience: it should be good news.

The task of the Christian school is to educate young people into the spiritual dimension of their lives. By spiritual I do not wish to draw a distinction between mind and spirit: between the process of achieving spiritual growth on the one hand and achieving mental, moral and affective growth on the other. The spiritual dimension deals with the most essential elements of peoples lives; with what makes them come alive, be most themselves, their very breath as it were. Human beings are endowed with reason and their surprise dignity lies in the intellect: in their ability to think, to learn, to know, to make conscious decisions, to communicate, to love and to act freely and maturely in their relationships with others and with God. Christian education is education for maturity and freedom and seeks to provide people with meaning, with a reason for human existence which, according to Christ, is that all may be one in love as he and the Father are one. Christ sought to build a genuinely human community where, with God as Father, all men and women could live as brothers and sisters in justice and love. The school's purpose is to make its contribution towards this objective by creating a learning community that educates students for maturity and freedom by pursuing truth in all areas of curricular and extra-curricular activities. The object of this pursuit is not merely the acquisition of cultural capital for selfish gain but so that students will acquire a faith that, in the spirit of Christ, will motivate them to live life to the full and help build a world of love and justice.

Pursuing truth means developing the ability to wonder and to think correctly and this is not automatic or inevitable; it does not just come with age but has to be encouraged and developed. Thinking is something I do, not something that someone else can do for me. How many students wish it were otherwise! The way I think affects the quality of my personal and social life and it can lead me astray. If, for example, I think that other people are always responsible for the way I feel and act or that others can never be trusted, I am indulging in ways of thinking that prevent me from living life to the full. Such ideas can, on close examination, be seen to be basically false but that does not stop them from being popular misconceptions. When a teacher enables me to find the truth about the source of my own emotions or helps build up a climate of trust s(h)e is a bearer of good news for I am being liberated from ways of thinking that dehumanise life.

Young children are always asking why. They have an instinctive desire for knowledge and truth. The genuine educator is someone who fosters this habit of inquiry at all levels of the educational process. Education is not only about acquiring knowledge but, in that process, learning how to learn, how to use one's mind so that it continually strives after truth. A merely passive, receptive attitude of mind that accepts uncritically whatever is proposed to it and in particular that form of 'learning' that accepts facts as lumps of undigested information to be retained unaltered by sheer force of memory until such time as it is regurgitated in an examination and then quickly forgotten, can hardly be called education.

To learn means that I adopt an attitude of suspended judgment towards new information until, by critical study, I am satisfied that what has been proposed to me is true either because the authority for it convinces me or because I have been shown and appreciate how the new information is related to what I already know or follows clearly from it, fits in with it and so convinces me. All the time I am making a mental map of reality which needs constant revision as I discover new continents of knowledge, or this or that island appears and has to be incorporated into what I already know. To learn is essentially an active, positive attitude that checks, examines and scrutinises a fact or statement until one is certain of its truth. In this way I make the matter my own: it has been digested, assimilated and become part of me.

A good teacher tries to help students achieve critical awareness which is not just a matter of doubting for doubting's sake but an awareness that truth is the most important thing in life; truth about oneself, others, God and his creation, and that falsehood is the worst evil and the degrees of falsehood – misunderstandings, prejudices, misconceptions – are degrees of evil to be overcome.

The ideal of truth is not innate. Because of human apathy, I have to learn to search out truth, whether about myself, others or creation and this is a slow and painful business in the face of which my basic apathy or sinfulness can put up fierce barriers of resistance. One major task of the educator is, by example, to help students overcome these barriers. Unless the conviction that truth is to be sought is a real and personal one there is the danger that critical awareness may degenerate into a sterile doubting for doubting's sake which is destructive of all learning.

Teaching methods that lead to a critical, independent attitude of mind can also lead to an undue reliance on my own limited powers, to a lessening of respect for all authority and to intellectual pride. But if I set truth as my ideal I will soon come to realise, through my frequent mistakes, that to achieve truth there is no glib, dilettante method that can substitute for real effort.

Education is about encouraging wonder, the pursuit of truth and the gaining of knowledge as a life-long process. As a teacher I try to tap into and encourage young people's innate wonder and their natural desire to know. I do not kill that desire by using the young person's mind simply as a dumping ground for useless facts. Genuine knowledge is to the mind and heart what food is to the body and such knowledge is gained by asking questions: new and appropriate questions. Once someone has learned to continually ask relevant questions, she has learned how to learn and no one can keep her from learning what she wants or needs to know. An educator is not someone who get's the stuff in at all costs, but someone who adapts educational practice so as to foster inquisitiveness of mind rather than demanding mere acceptance. When pupils take a teacher at his word and question as much as they can, he takes delight in his pupils' growth. The good teacher encourages students to be analytic in their approach to any new truth, to examine it to see if it relates to the knowledge the pupil has in order to understand and appreciate its coherence.

Growth in knowledge has to be a gradual development, not a forced growth, and the teacher knows she has succeeded when her students need her no longer!

The present system of education is based largely on the transmission model of education and, for many pupils, is simply boring, to use their own vocabulary. By and large pupils do not learn by doing (the best way to learn is to teach, it is said) but sit passively behind desks for hours on end. They are not encouraged to learn through reflecting on their own experience or cope with the vast amount of information pouring daily from the media, or helped to sort out the important from the trivial, the useful from the useless, the true from the false. When pupils do think for themselves and express their opinions they often face admonition, moralising and criticism. Pupils are not helped to grow in the art of decision making or enabled to appreciate and value the world through history, the arts, music, painting, sculpture and drama, subjects largely regarded as peripheral with mathematics and science taking centre stage.

Intellectual stimulation is often lacking, especially for weaker students. Their natural desire to know, to wonder in the face of the world, is cut off with an early introduction to concentrating on what is 'on the course'. Like the parent who tires of answering the constant questioning of a child, eventually telling him to be quiet, the system encourages passive listening and absorption of material and discourages questioning or argument about what is presented. The system does not encourage pupils to try to discover things for themselves and so they switch off. Because of the demands of the examination system, pupils are not able to learn at their own pace and teachers, knowing full-well that some things come easier to some pupils than to others, do not have the time to cater for the real needs of the so-called 'slow learner' because they have to 'cover the course'. Only the student who can absorb material fast and then find enough stimulation to enquire outside the normal boundaries flourishes in such a system.

Growth in knowledge can be achieved in a far more interesting and stimulating way. Secondary education can be a voyage of discovery. Knowledge comes when I step back mentally from my world and critically question all that I have learned or been taught, not being critical for criticism's sake, but in order to discover the truth about myself and the world I inhabit. Education is not simply a transfer of facts from teacher or pupil but a joint effort where teacher and pupil investigate together so that the truth may prevail. To be educated means that I am helped to gain mental distance from what I had previously taken for granted and enabled, through questioning and investigation, to discover the truth for myself, or I am presented with new data and helped to see where it fits into what I already know, into my map of reality. New data is presented as a problem for investigation and what is called for is thought. In this way of looking at education, the teacher is mainly concerned with asking questions, looking for opinions or trying to clarify matters with the aim of enabling students to think and clarify matters for themselves. As teacher, I ask how, why and where is the connection? I look for reasons, causes, meanings so that students can find their own answers.

Of course presenting new material, memorisation and repetition do have a part to play. It is necessary to memorise things and repeat them so that student can consolidate their discoveries but the overall aim is not to store unrelated facts but to enlarge the pupils map of reality. Exaggerating the importance of information storage is a hangover from earlier days when traditional wisdom was the result of countless ages of trial and error and each new generation could not risk its survival by forgetting it. In the age of the computer and quick retrieval systems such storage has become redundant.

Education is to be measured not by the amount of information students remember but by their ability to wonder, question, reason, appreciate, think critically and constantly revise their map of reality. Once students show confidence in their ability to learn; rely more on their own judgments, while ready to modify their first opinions; have respect for evidence and logic; be cautious and provisional in answering problems but ready to test out their conclusions in action, then they are on the road to being truly educated. One of the great obstacles to genuine education is the idea that large amounts of information are to be poured into relatively blank young minds. Experience shows that such a method does not encourage life-long questioning and the pursuit of truth but makes for boredom and 'switch-off'.

Teachers may well object that they cannot afford to waste time letting pupils discover in hours what they could be told in minutes. But they may be looking at things from the wrong perspective. As a teacher I may lecture a class for forty minutes, give out many ideas and summarise things that would take hours to present to a class as problems for them to investigate. My class might even be interesting. My students may listen to me for part of the time, take notes and even remember something of what I said, though, as most teachers know, a lot of what is said in class tends to 'go in one ear and out of the other'! Mere listening is not the most effective way to learn. Where students are presented with a problem and invited to become actively involved in questioning it and investigating it at their own pace, learning will or course take longer but it will be real learning.

'But we have to cover the course. Pupils have to pass their Leaving Cert!' True. But learning could be much more effective if what was assessed in public examinations was students ability to ask relevant and appropriate questions and to think and communicate their ideas about the sciences, mathematics, business, the world of language, history, the arts, social affairs, politics and economics. If the public examination system measured their ability to investigate, to synthesise and to use information effectively; to lay out rational arguments logically and communicate them effectively; to wonder and appreciate beauty, to search for truth, then society would have a better yardstick by which to judge a person's capabilities, rather than relying on the massive recall of unrelated bits of information.

Students' boredom with much that happens in our present educational system may be a sign of Grace, a sign calling for salvation: salvation from the death-bearing philosophy that economic success is the answer to life's problems and that education's primary role is to serve economic interests rather than human development.

CHAPTER 14

Witnessing to Faith

Faith should clearly have pride of place in a Christian school. We have already noted the many obstacles placed in its path by modern Irish society.

The danger for schools is that Christian faith is simply relegated to religious education classes and hence the spiritual and the secular worlds become divorced from each other and faith no longer 'speaks' to young people for it seems to be in a realm completely separate from their other 'more important' subjects. 'There are no points for R.E. in the Leaving Cert,' as one parent put it!

Faith speaks about the continuous action of God in peoples' lives. The impulse towards becoming more loving and self-giving, more human and humane, towards overcoming ignorance and prejudice and striving after truth, is one impulse of God's gracious activity in the world which Christian teachers need to make explicit and to foster in their students. God's creative action is to be found in mathematics, geography, science, literature, history, art and music as well as in R.E. classes. When the two worlds become totally separate, the message of Christ is betrayed.

One way to help students find God in all things is by fostering the habit of prayer. Indeed this is perhaps more crucial than doctrine and dogma at this stage of their development and should be the main topic of their religion classes. Prayer is to faith what dialogue is to a successful marriage or any lasting friendship. If prayer is lacking in a person's life, faith will soon wither. It is not just a matter of 'saying prayers' but of establishing and maintaining a relationship with God. Today's society is a very superficial one that often pollutes the mind with trivia. Some dimension of stillness, some experience of inwardness, some effort at prayer is necessary if people are to counteract this pollution. To pray is to relax into the reality of God's presence and love. Knowing God's presence, people will be able to love from God and from a deeper part of themselves. People need to find ways, different for each individual, of relaxing into Love's presence with them and within them and within the whole of creation for God is present in history and science, in mathematics and art, in music and football, as well as in you and me and in every relationship.

By the time young people come to secondary school they have reached a time of searching for identity through relationships and through emotional solidarity with peer groups. Prayer and liturgy should reflect these preoccupations. Faith at this stage is groping, unreflective and inarticulate: a sort of pre-decision stage. It is only when people are in their twenties and thirties, often after becoming distanced from the conventions of religion, that they can assume a new responsibility for choices, and faith becomes an explicit conviction and commitment, able to swim against the social tide. At its core, faith is a more personal sense of Christ that helps one to become an alert and adult believer. The painful transition from faith in adolescence to faith in adulthood is typically nourished by learning to pray more deeply from the scriptures, by the support of some community of believers and by undertaking some regular service of others in need. All three elements need to be taken into account by schools if young people are to mature in faith in a healthy way.

If Christian faith is to be Good News for students, it has to be experienced in and through good relationships and good communication between teachers and students. It has to be experienced through the witness of teachers themselves in their own lives. The action of God in all dimensions of learning has to be made explicit not only in words but also in the way teachers and pupils interact. Above all, the reality of faith must be demonstrated by the time and attention given by staff to the weakest and poorest in the school.

Faith must then be expressed in relationships and through the sacramental, liturgical and prayerful expression of those relationships and what they mean. Any sacramental or liturgical expression should take account of where young people are at and of their preoccupations.

Faith has also to be lived-out in relationships of justice and service, both within the school community and in some form of service to those outside. People cannot say they believe in God and not allow that to change the way they live, they way they want society to be. To be a Christian is to be committed to changing the world towards justice for all, and indeed of questioning one's own lifestyle in this respect. The purpose of asking students to provide some service to those in need outside the school is not so that they will change the world but so that, through experience and reflection, they can learn about the reality of life for those marginalised in our society and realise that their work at school may one day enable them to build a more just society.

A nineteen-year-old girl speaking to a group of school Principals about what young people wanted from school, made the following observations. 'Young people live lives of mixed emotions. They are in a period of transition. They experience feelings of rebellion. They want to be "in control" and so they are often anti-religion, which seems to impose so many obligations and restrictions. Young people have very inadequate religious ideas and often have a fear of perfection, of feeling inadequate because they cannot live up to the very high ideals religious faith calls for. Sometimes their family background is hostile to religion.

'Young people are basically good in themselves. They often suffer mental abuse at home or from their friends. They are put down, talked at, ordered about by parents or teachers, jeered at and knocked socially by their peers. They are inward looking. They mostly believe in God but like to be seen as "cool dudes". They are shy about their faith and afraid that if they were to express it, it would ruin their image. They often lack opportunities to express their faith. They lack a spirituality. They desire leadership.

'Young people want to be loved. They need a setting in which they can experience their dignity as persons: an atmosphere of sincere respect and friendship. They need to experience Christian values through their interpersonal experiences.

'They want teachers to be professional with them but not "into power". They want their teachers to be human; to talk about themselves; to be open and to share. They want teachers to be prepared to take a risk and be vulnerable. They want to be given their own time and space. They want teachers to be impartial, to be fair. They want them to smile and acknowledge them. They want to be "in control", so they want discipline in order to know the parameters in which they can rebel! They want teachers to be gentle. They want them to be kind but firm. They do not want a relationship of fear but one of encouragement.'

Young people need good relationships with believing teachers and parents. They also need some experience of prayer. Bad relationships in the home or school and an absence of prayerful experience seem to be a formula for creating a nominal faith or unbelief.

The greatest service parents and teachers can give to young people is to spend time with them and have a good relationship with them. Homes or schools filled with supposed religion, but empty of love, simply turn young people off religion. It is not that parents and teachers should always be talking about God, but that young people experience God (Love) through the whole atmosphere and the values that pervade home and school.

Adults also need to recognise their own needs. Simply going to Church and leading good lives does not make for a mature Christian. They, too, need to grow in inwardness, in prayer, in understanding the faith and in some challenge to their lifestyle. If adults do not do this, young people will not see the full reality of Christian faith lived out in the world.

Schools are being challenged by the individualism, consumerism and pragmatism of Irish society. If educators are to counteract these influences, they need to find new forms of community and of prayer, new ways of understanding the faith and new ways of commitment and of living out the faith in service, especially to the poorest and most marginalised. By doing this they can find new meaning and a sense of purpose in life. They will be following in the Master's footsteps and have more to offer young people than a lifeless philosophy of 'getting and spending'. They will be true bearers of Good News.

The challenge is no easy one but then Jesus of Nazareth never promised us a rose garden – only the Cross!